Hands-on Technology

Dedicated to Brian,
without whose patience and support my work
and this book would not have been possible.

Hands-on Technology

Iris Kathrynne Idle

Stanley Thornes (Publishers)

First published in 1991 by:
Stanley Thornes (Publishers) Ltd
Old Station Drive
Leckhampton
Cheltenham GL53 0DN

British Cataloguing in Publication Data
    Idle, Iris
    Hands-on technology
    I. Title
    372. 3

ISBN 0–7487-1296–8

Computer page make up Penny Mills, Coventry
Printed and bound in Great Britain at The Bath Press, Avon

Contents

Acknowledgements

The author wishes to thank Christopher for the line illustrations, David Jinks for introducing her to technology, John Pegge for his encouragement and support throughout her work in Primary Technology in Sheffield, and to acknowledge the help of many colleagues in Sheffield, Barnsley and Leeds schools.

Note: The technology Attainment Targets referred to throughout are from the DES document *Technology in the National Curriculum*, HMSO, 1990. The Attainment Targets for maths, science and English referred to in the chart on pages 84 to 89 are from the DES documents *Maths in the National Curriculum*, HMSO, 1989, and *English in the National Curriculum*, HMSO, 1990.

Introduction

My aim, in writing this book, is to help class teachers to make technology with young children an integral part of their curriculum – both exciting and rewarding.

I have a wide range of experience of classroom teaching throughout the primary school, and have spent a number of years working alongside children, teachers, students and parents as a technology adviser and trainer. By sharing this experience, I hope to help my fellow teachers to integrate technology in a cross-curricular way into good primary practice. We should not see the National Curriculum technology document as a threat to our good teaching, but rather as a guide to identify and broaden the technology work already taking place in our classrooms.

This book identifies, with examples, areas where technology work is already established, and provides many starting points for practical, problem-solving experiences to meet the requirements of the National Curriculum.

The book can be used in a variety of ways. It can provide ideas and practical techniques for work in technology. I hope it will also lead you to consider your present style of teaching. Do you try to develop the individual child's thinking, reasoning and problem-solving skills? Or do you tend to direct the children to one 'right' solution? If your honest answer to the last question is 'yes', then you might need to think about how you will teach technology successfully. In these pages you will find some simple suggestions to help you.

Children cannot go through life in groups of 20; it is therefore essential that we give each individual child the opportunity to become independent in their thinking. We should encourage them to attempt and solve problems confidently, and to realise that mistakes are stepping stones along the path of learning, not to be looked upon as failures but rather as challenges.

Encouraging children to plan and make their own solutions to design opportunities is the basis of good technology teaching.

Perhaps we might all ask ourselves the following question: 'Is the education package which we had when we were at school the right package for today's child facing tomorrow's world?'

I don't think that any of us can give the answer 'yes' to that. Therefore, I hope that the contents of this book will help you to equip today's children with the relevant skills and experiences needed to fit them for the fast changing world into which they will go.

Part 1   Young Children and Technology

The first section of my book draws your attention to the understanding of technology and its natural place in the learning of young children. It shows clearly that if children are given opportunities within the classroom, they will surprise you with their ingenuity, creativity and problem-solving skills.

1   Young Children and Technology

Design and technological capability in the early years, as specified in the National Curriculum, is concerned with developing the ability of young children to identify, through exploring familiar learning contexts – the classroom, home, locality – various needs and opportunities for design-related activities. The teacher's task is to encourage children to develop their ideas (AT 1), first through discussion then by recording, using sketches and paintings (AT 2). Experience of simple tools, construction kits and appropriate materials enables the children to turn these first ideas and designs into artefacts, systems or environments (AT 3). This demonstration of their own solutions to the tasks chosen will develop their understanding of

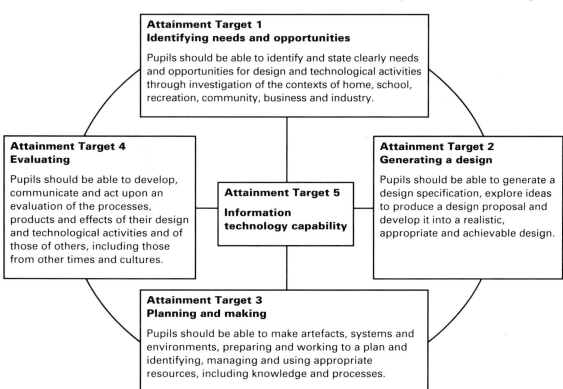

Attainment Target 1
Identifying needs and opportunities

Pupils should be able to identify and state clearly needs and opportunities for design and technological activities through investigation of the contexts of home, school, recreation, community, business and industry.

Attainment Target 4
Evaluating

Pupils should be able to develop, communicate and act upon an evaluation of the processes, products and effects of their design and technological activities and of those of others, including those from other times and cultures.

Attainment Target 5

Information technology capability

Attainment Target 2
Generating a design

Pupils should be able to generate a design specification, explore ideas to produce a design proposal and develop it into a realistic, appropriate and achievable design.

Attainment Target 3
Planning and making

Pupils should be able to make artefacts, systems and environments, preparing and working to a plan and identifying, managing and using appropriate resources, including knowledge and processes.

Department of Education and Science and the Welsh Office, *Technology in the National Curriculum*, HMSO, March 1990.

how things work, and how they can effect change in the world around them. Discussion and self assessment of their results lead the children to modify, redesign or accept their individual solutions (AT 4).

Children's technological experience

Technological activities involve a natural broadening of the children's experience. Because technology occurs naturally in many subject areas, it invites a cross-curricular approach. We can find opportunities throughout the curriculum for children to think things out for themselves, by identifying and solving, by designing and making, their own solutions to real problems. Such an approach helps children to the understanding that knowledge and skills in using a variety of materials and tools can bring about change and improvement in their own environment.

When very young children play at home, they are frequently employing, at a basic level, skills and thinking processes which are central to later work in CDT. They manipulate toy bricks into patterns or structures, press into service all kinds of containers and pieces of material, use objects made for one purpose as substitutes for others with completely different uses and constantly revise what they have made as new ideas strike them; as better materials come to hand; and as they learn from their own experience.
CDT from 5-16. Curriculum Matters 9, DES, 1987

Learning should be fun. Young children are naturally very curious and do not need to be pushed to learn; rather they need to be stimulated and receive positive encouragement for each small step forward. Children possess a fresh, playful attitude and, as teachers, we should work to keep this alive. Nursery schools are so often successful because there is more time for play; as children get older, this is lost. Surely, in our planning and approach in the classroom we should be able to keep this enjoyment and infectiousness for learning alive!

Children starting school arrive from a wide variety of backgrounds

Practical, activity-based learning is the best way for children to develop their problem-solving skills.

which provide an equally wide variety of experiences. For example, one child who has been bathed in language may have had little opportunity for manipulating materials; another child may have had lots of opportunities to play with materials but be linguistically deprived. Our task as teachers is to ascertain the individual needs of the children in the class.

It is fair to assume that young children starting school may possess some, if not all, of the following 'basic' skills and concepts:
- perception
- imagination
- inquisitiveness
- linguistic skills
- an elementary level of manipulative skills
- a certain level of social skills.

How can these skills be used and developed?

We all know that young children learn best through a 'hands on' approach based on first-hand experience, with activities designed to cater for an individual, spontaneous response. It is through exploration, investigation and discovery that children learn about their immediate surroundings and the world in which they live. Our task as teachers is to create the classroom environment (see Appendix 1) in which this activity-based learning can take place and (with the sensitive intervention of an adult when appropriate) lead children to develop and refine concepts and skills.

It is important that technological experiences are included in this enterprise, since it is through such practical, problem-solving activities that children are most likely to gain an understanding of the world and develop what can simply be described as 'mechanical common sense'. That is, an understanding of materials, mechanical functions and elementary engineering concepts. Opportunities should be created which enable children to experience mechanical principles such as pull, push, twist, balance, screw, spring, lever, press, lift, using a variety of materials and by investigating and playing with toys. Included in this activity, children should be encouraged to investigate familiar objects where energy is stored, controlled and released, so gaining an insight into the forces resulting from using water, weights, sand, wind and themselves as energy sources.

Model-making with construction kits – the beginnings of a mechanical understanding.

The wide range of construction kits available for young children will enable them, when ready, to make things move and stop moving. They will also give them the opportunity to explore a variety of mechanisms and use basic components such as wheels, gears and rollers. Kits such as Lego, Duplo, Mobilo, Bauplay, Tactic, Brio, Reo-Click, First Gear and Plastic Meccano are an excellent resource for this activity (see Chapter 8).

During this work, young children should become familiar with an increasing technical vocabulary; for example, wheel, roller, axle, washer, pin, screw, etc. They should be able to use these words where appropriate to tell others what they have done or are going to do, giving reasons for their choices (AT 1). They should be given opportunities to ask questions, seek answers and discuss and evaluate their ideas with the teacher and with other children (AT 4).

2 From Simple Beginnings – Progression in Technology

I would like to preface the practical sections of this book by explaining how I first became involved in technology (after training as a musician) and by sharing with you my first technological activities with my class of 8-year-olds.

I was deputy head of an open-plan primary school when two of my colleagues went for a one-day course at the teacher's centre to look at CDT (as it was then called) with young children. They came back and both said that it was the course for me. When two members of staff tell you this, you have to do something about it, so off I went when the course was next advertised. Before this course I had worked with children with 'collectable' materials to make various models (artefacts) linked with our topic work, but with little success. The boxes fell apart, they were not rigid, extra Sellotape and Blu-tak failed to secure them. This resulted in both the children and myself becoming frustrated and returning to fabrics, clay, paint and other materials with which we knew we could have success. The course introduced me to new techniques and I realised that I could share these skills with the children and broaden the package of education which they were experiencing. The following pages explain exactly what happened.

First experiences – with 8- to 9-year-olds

The children in the second year juniors were in the midst of studying a project entitled 'The Open Road'. This was based on a BBC programme which followed the development of roads from the early Stone Age through to today's motorways.

Individual books were made by the children covering all aspects of their topic work but there was no three-dimensional development in their art work. Previous attempts to make models using corrugated cardboard, boxes, clay and other media had resulted in little long-term success, but as a result of my one-day CDT course, I returned to school full of enthusiasm and new construction techniques with which to broaden the children's practical curriculum.

I first looked at the classroom to find a corner in which to collect together the simple tools and materials needed: hacksaws, bench hooks, a hand drill, 8 mm square wood of different lengths, 4.5 mm dowel, thin and thick card, Marvin Medium glue. There was already in the room a small woodwork bench, which had been used for anything but woodwork! This was an ideal place on which to store the tools. It also had a small vice so that the children could hold firmly the pieces they wished to cut.

The children were curious to know why I had not been at school the previous day. I explained that I had been on a course and showed them the chassis and cube I had made (see pages 105–113). They were very impressed and asked, 'When are we going to do something like this?' I had to be a little patient at this stage because I did not wish to force anything into the curriculum that was not relevant to the work taking place.

The opportunity to integrate the techniques into classroom work did not come through their topic work as expected but during a mathematics lesson. The children were working with Primary Scottish Maths and Andrew reached the question, 'How many sides has a cube?' As I had made a cube on the in-service day, I gathered together six children who were at that stage in mathematics, talked with them about the cube, using the one that I had made as an example, and they set off to make one for themselves.

Teaching skills

This was the moment when I taught skills. I must stress that the teaching of skills, although necessary to enable children to successfully solve technological activities, does not in itself constitute technology. The children were taught how to use a hacksaw, bench hook and materials safely. Through the need for accuracy and a practical use for right angles (for the cardboard corners they had to cut), maths skills were being developed. The children were highly motivated by the challenge of using a new technique in practical work.

When the first six children had made their cubes, they taught the next six. If children have fully understood the process through which they have gone, they can pass on their expertise to others. This was the way the skills were passed by one group to the next until all 26 children had made a cube.

A new skill in action

These were hung from the classroom ceiling to be viewed from many angles.

Applying skills

I asked the first child to finish his cube whether he could think of a way to use this technique to link with the topic on 'The Open Road'. He quickly replied, 'I'm going to make a Model T Ford!' You can imagine my reaction. I had only made a cube, however could I cope with a Model T Ford? Luckily, instead of telling the child that it was impossible, I said, 'And how in the world do you think you can do that?' His reply was given in

Model T Ford

such detail that I realised he knew exactly what he wanted and that I wasn't going to have to do it. (Thank goodness – I really wasn't at that stage myself!) I simply told him to get on with it. I realised soon afterwards that all I had had to do was set him off on the path of discovery and give him the freedom to design and make his model.

Other children followed his lead, choosing various vehicles from a simple trolley to modern fire engines and a Lamborghini racing car, until the whole class was engrossed. As this activity started in May and it was only two months away from the end of the school year, a lot of time was devoted to this work. I was concerned about this as open evening was looming, when I would have to justify to parents the work the children had been doing. To many onlookers these activities could appear to be play, but standing and analysing what was taking place left me in no doubt that the time given to this practical activity was justified.

The children were totally involved in purposeful activities. They were developing thinking and reasoning skills, language skills, mathematics and science skills, and social skills, all through problem solving. They were handling and gaining experience of using a wide variety of materials. Some children became leaders, and those not successful academically achieved real success through this practical approach. They were only too happy to share materials, equipment and ideas in order to solve their problems. One child, who had a serious behavioural problem and for whom all agencies concerned had recommended special education, became successfully integrated when the other children found him a source of help and not a hindrance.

I did not have all the answers; when two bulbs were not very bright on the Model T Ford, help had to be sought. But I learned alongside the children that there was a difference between wiring in series and wiring in parallel. I also realised that this was part of a process of learning in which the children were in control and the teacher stood back. The children were responsible for their tools, materials, storage of half finished models, etc, and thus for their own learning situation. The first steps in technology had been made.

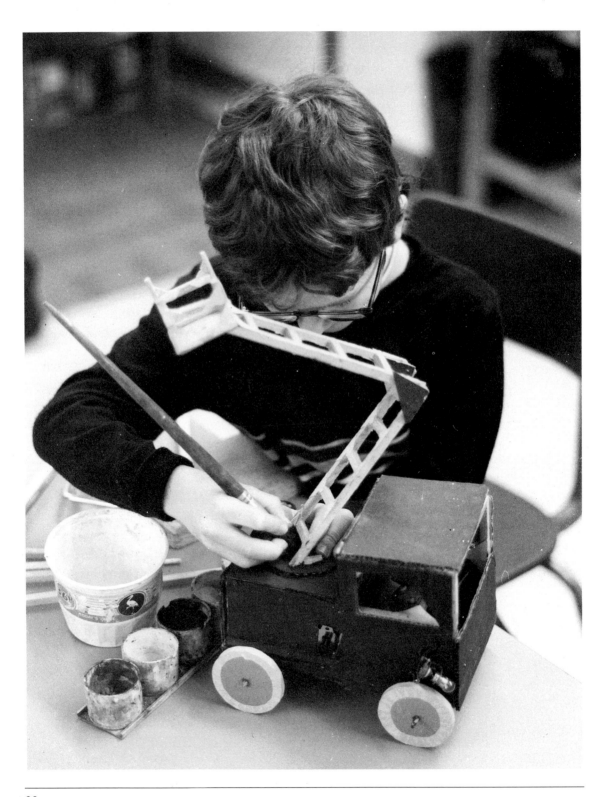

Opposite: Children are highly motivated by realising their own ideas.

Parents' evening arrived and the children proudly displayed their models. I discovered that they had told their parents a great deal about their work, discussing these activities far more than a piece of English or maths, so that some of the parents knew much more about the problems the children had encountered, and many of these had been solved in discussion at the tea table. Parents who had not come to an open evening before arrived to see the children's work; their involvement and co-operation was a direct result of the motivation of the children.

When the models were finished, the children presented their work to the class and talked about how they had made their models. They assessed their results very honestly. The boy who made the Model T Ford said, 'I wouldn't make it that way if I made it again. The steering wheel hits the roof and the seat is too high!'

Linking this work (which took place in 1984) to the National Curriculum technology document and the four Attainment Targets, it is interesting to see that the children, after being taught the initial skills of using the tools and materials safely, identified their own need linked with their topic (AT 1), made their models (AT 3), evaluated them (AT 4) and then, after the making was completed, were happy to sketch and write a description showing how they had started and gone through each stage to the finished model (AT 2). This clearly shows that young children, given the relevant opportunities, experience naturally the design process covered by the National Curriculum Attainment Targets. This first activity also showed that children need lots of experience of 'making', using a variety of materials, before they know what the materials will do and before they can design for their use.

Developing skills with 9- to 10-year-olds

It was at this stage that I was seconded from my deputy headship to be a member of a national project looking at technology with young children. This enabled me to spend part

Opposite: The horse gin. Once basic techniques have been mastered, children are ingenious in adapting them to each new technological situation.

of my time with teachers throughout the country and the remainder of my time was spent in Sheffield working with both teachers and children.

The opportunity arose to observe these children over the next two years of their primary school life. Part of their work in the third year involved a residential visit to Derbyshire. Only 20 children could be accommodated at one time so the year group was split into two groups, each covering the same programme. The first group visited the lead mine at Matlock and saw a broken horse gin. They returned to school and, as part of their topic, asked if they could make a working model of this gin.

This was the first time that the children had worked in a group, two boys and three girls. There was much discussion about the horse gin. Its purpose was to lift tubs out of the lead mine. The children decided to make a winding device first, rather like the top of a well, then they had to design their horse gin. They went straight to materials and worked in two smaller groups, one group building the framework and the others making the large paper plate pulley and the two smaller pulleys. They worked on quite a large scale, using a wider range of wood and previously acquired skills. The children were now very confident with the wood techniques and were happy to venture into real problem solving. They approached the task with confidence and produced a working model with artwork, creative written work, photography and poetry to support it.

The second group of 20 to visit the lead mine found that the water pump was not working, so they decided to try and make a working model. They worked in small groups, some of girls, some of boys, some mixed. Their designs were first thought out by sketching simple drawings in order that they could think out and plan before the 'making' stage was reached.

It was interesting to watch the development of their thinking. The first models made had the sole aim of lifting the water from the mine – when the water reached the top of the conveyor belt or plastic pipe, it went straight back down the mine. They tested their models many times in water and found, to their dismay,

Will the glue hold in water? It is important that, through testing, children evaluate and modify their first ideas.

that PVA glue dissolved in water. Should I have told them this before they built? Their first-hand experience led naturally into an investigation of glues to find which glue would have been most suitable for the task. The models were rescued from the water, dried out and polyurethane varnished so that they could be tested again.

Once the children had found that they could lift the water from the lead mine, the next task was to divert it away from the top of the mine. Eventually, they used plastic pipes. They did not find a suitable glue to fix two plastic pipes together, but discovered that a whole packet of teacher's Blu-tak worked!

Their choice of materials had now broadened: clay, bandage, beads, plastic tubes and pipes, and all manner of other things suddenly appeared in order to help them solve the problem. There is never just one correct solution; children are able to develop their own ideas to produce several, all of which might fulfil the task required.

Real problems and their solutions – at 10 to 11 years

Industry year, 1986, provided the next stimulus for the children. They decided to look at the tools which they were using and find out how they had developed. They looked back in history to

The design stage

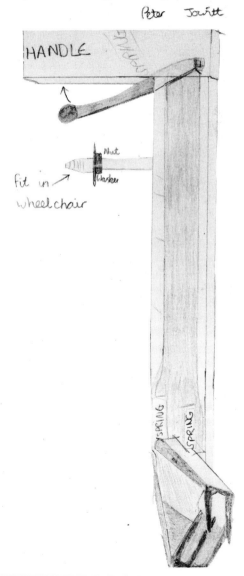

Working models of gardening tools for use from a wheelchair – solutions to a real problem

tools used by early man and this led to an interest in how they might develop tools for someone in need.

The school secretary's mother, who was severely handicapped with rheumatism, visited school and the children questioned her about life in a wheelchair and the tasks which she found difficult. The children listed these and went off to the drawing boards to sketch some ideas. For the first time the children were really designing before making. This had taken almost two years from their first experience of making a cube.

Various difficulties were investigated. Having a shower as a handicapped person proved to be a problem which the children solved very easily. They made a model using a shoe box which they stood on its smallest end to represent a shower cubicle.

They stuck a yoghurt pot lid into the base, full of holes, to make a shower for use by able-bodied people. Then they turned a yoghurt pot over and twisted that into the lid so that a handicapped person could sit on it and have a shower. Telephones took on different shapes so that someone with limited use of their hand could use them. Some children looked at a special screwdriver for a person with only one hand. Two children looked at the difficulties of gardening from a wheelchair and developed two ideas for gardening tools, one with detachable ends for various jobs in the garden and another for weeding.

Unfortunately, there was insufficient time for the children to finish their models before they left for secondary school. The teacher who was working with them invited a tool manufacturer into school to see the work which they had produced and to talk to them about how real materials would be tested to choose those most suitable for their ideas. They learned how their tools would be manufactured, packaged and marketed, seeing the whole process from their first ideas to the finished article.

In conclusion

In two years, the children had gone a long way towards being able to identify needs, generate a design, plan and make and finally to evaluate. The whole design process was a part of their approach to learning, not a linear process but one which could go forwards, back, round and round until the final product was to their satisfaction. They were well equipped with skills, concepts and attitudes to face tomorrow's technological world, yet all this developed in two years from a simple starting point with simple tools and materials. Surely it is our task as educators to give every child these opportunities from the earliest age possible in order that we can equip them with the skills for living, working and enriching life in tomorrow's world.

Part 2   Before You Start

It is important that, before children embark on technological activities, careful thought has been given to the organisation of time, space, materials and equipment. The following two chapters will help your planning which, in turn, will enable the children to achieve success.

3   Preparing for Technology

As with any curriculum area, good organisation is the key to the successful introduction and development of technology in your classroom. On the next pages I raise some practical issues for you to consider in your preparation.

Time and opportunity

Trying to cover everything in the curriculum will always impose time restrictions on the primary teacher. However, in planning for technological work, you should not let these restrictions dictate or limit the type of activities your children undertake. Before you start organising your time and activities for technology, you might like to consider the following points:

- A practical activity cannot be fitted into a set amount of time; a degree of flexibility is necessary.
- While children are motivated, they should be encouraged to continue (though we should be aware of varying concentration spans within the group).
- Open-ended situations which are related to the children's existing experiences will enable creative skills to be developed.
- Children need thinking time; it should not cause anxiety if they appear at moments not to be active.
- We should try to set work that makes demands and challenges the children.
- We should encourage children to analyse what they are doing from an early age.
- It is a good idea to give children the responsibility for getting materials ready and clearing away so that they become familiar with the materials available and their storage. (A 'treasure hunt' familiarisation game may be a good idea to collect items and return them to their home.)

Flexibility is the key. Children may need anything from a few minutes to a few months for their task. In organising technology activities, try to allow the time and opportunity for:

- exploration of materials
- handling tools
- finding appropriate materials
- information retrieval and research
- experimentation
- learning and practice of skills
- leaving work until another time
- thinking about the problem
- modification
- discussion
- development of concepts
- analysis of their own work
- reflection
- evaluation of the quality of work.

It can be difficult to come to terms with the amount of time children require in order to achieve success and a sense of achievement. It is, however, important to realise that while children are engaged in technological activities, they are also developing skills in the following curriculum areas:

- language, spoken and written
- mathematics
- science
- history
- geography
- art and design.

If these are added to the reasoning, thinking and problem-solving skills, the social skills of sharing ideas, materials and helping each other, most people would agree that the length of time given to technology is benefiting the whole curriculum package.

Timetable management

Technology should be a part of daily activities within the classroom of very young children. A corner equipped with small tools, nails, a bench and large pieces of wood will enable

Children need to become familiar with the safe use of tools and new skills before starting on technology activities.

children to start to develop the many skills required in this area of the curriculum. The children may spend a considerable amount of time each day working with a variety of materials and construction kits. As the children get older and their concentration span increases, they will be more able to work for longer periods.

The time available has to be thought through as a whole-school policy. It may be possible for one afternoon each week to be used for technological activities. Another possibility is that once children start on an activity, they are given the time to go through the whole process of planning, making and evaluating. This may be one whole day or even two. If the process of learning through which we wish the children to go is to be possible, time has to be made available. If two days are used for this work then perhaps the children's next experience will not be for two or three weeks. The time factor depends very much upon the way in which a school plans its timetable, whether the class teacher is responsible for their own timetable or whether a specialist teacher is taking charge of the technology activities within the school.

I hope that teaching staff will discuss the place of technology within their school and not attach it to the curriculum as a specialist subject. To achieve real success, it has to be seen as a broadening of our present integrated teaching approach. Schools need to address the balance of the timetable to suit their working methods and the children in their care. This discussion will enable them to include technology and will also enable them to 'brainstorm' each other when they have problems.

Within each LEA, there is an Advisor or Inspector for Technology and also advisory teachers for science/technology. Teachers must feel that they can use these additional resources. They are usually based at the teachers centres. Specialist consultants are also available to help with the organisation of technology within a school, looking at resources and running in-service days.

Group work

I do not suggest that technology activities be carried out with the whole class simultaneously. This could cause problems of supervision, resources and space. It is easier to work with a few children at a time, working individually or collaboratively.

We need to observe children closely in the classroom situation in order to assess whether they are ready to work within a group or pair. As professional teachers, we should never make assumptions that children have already achieved a certain level of social/intellectual development which enables group work to be collaborative.

Questions you can ask to determine whether children are ready to work in a group:

• Do they share the space amicably?
• Do they share materials?
• Do they refer to each other for advice and ideas as well as to an adult?
• Does this happen in other situations?

Try asking yourself the following questions before dividing the class into groups:

• Why do you want a number of children to work as a group?
• How are the groups formed – friendship, equal or mixed ability?
• Will the groups remain as they are throughout the whole course of the project?

Group work can only be effective if you have planned for it sufficiently, in advance. You should not try organising activities for a group of children who have never worked collaboratively before, but should build up to it gradually.

• In order to develop group skills, try to choose activities with 'working together' in mind. The task given must be appropriate for the group size, planned as a group activity, with one end product.
• Children need to explore things by themselves initially to gain confidence.

Individual work but within a small group may be a step towards collaborative group work.

- Children may be able to cope with working in pairs, although this may cause some problems with any finished product – who takes it home? Taking it home on a rota basis may solve this problem.
- Individual work but within a small group may be an appropriate stage towards group work.
- The time to begin group work may be when children begin to seek help from other children or peers. This development towards shared experiences can be enhanced by the groups working with an adult present.

Early stages in technology, where building simple shapes on a mirror is a suitable activity for both girls and boys.

Equal opportunities

When technological activities are being planned, it is important that these activities are relevant to the girls as well as the boys. In Part 1, Chapter 2, it was interesting to see that, in 'The Open Road' topic, many of the girls chose to make vehicles which required fabrics, either to cover the models or for use as seats. The boys tended to work with more rigid materials. The theme of the topic enabled both gender groups to enjoy the work and to be successful.

Technology has to be made exciting for both girls and boys. Designing their own bedrooms, looking at new ways in which to organise their classroom or cloakroom are all ideas which would appeal to all children. We don't have to think of technology in terms of things that move – bridges, cars and cranes. The important thing is to encourage all children to participate actively in a wide variety of technological problem-solving.

4   Materials and Storage

In the last chapter we looked at the kind of preparations we need to make before children are ready for the demands of problem-solving activities. In this chapter we will look at the kinds of materials your children will need for technology and how best to organise and store them.

Materials

The first step in technology for any child is the exploration of materials and tools. Very young children will benefit from the opportunity to experience a wide range of natural materials. Learning what can be done with different substances, their possibilities and limitations, will enable the children to put the materials to use in their first problem-solving activities.

Natural Materials

• sand	• wood (used with workbench, scaled-down tools and related materials)
• water	
• peat	• clay
• flour	• dough (coloured, cooked and uncooked)
• stones, rocks, pebbles and shells	
• leaves, twigs and cones	• any local material – chalk, coal, etc
• grass cuttings, hay, straw	
• salt	

What can I do with this? Very young children will benefit from the opportunity to experience a wide range of natural materials.

Extending opportunities

Activities can be extended by the addition of other materials, including manufactured equipment to develop imaginative play; for example, play people, animals and a variety of construction toys. Further exploration will be stimulated by the provision of scientific and mathematical apparatus - graded containers, tubing, water wheels, whisks, etc.

Technological activities may require lots of materials but many of these are the same kinds of 'collectables' that are familiar to all primary teachers (and parents!). It is a good idea to get children and parents involved from the start in getting hold of such materials, so that it is not left with you to get hold of, say, 20 empty cereal boxes at the last minute. It will also give you access to a much wider range of materials. The following lists include those 'free' items which should be easily available.

Collectable Materials

Plastic

- washing up liquid bottles
- pop bottles
- milk bottles
- yoghurt pots
- margarine tubs
- shopping bags
- polythene bags
- food trays
- table tennis balls
- plastic/rubber tubing
- plumbing bits and pieces
- beads
- cotton reels
- plastic lids from coffee jars, etc
- offcuts of perspex
- felt-tip pen tubes
- polystyrene tiles
- clothes pegs – hinged and dolly type
- nylon line
- tape spools
- old records
- lolly sticks
- drinking straws
- foam pipe lagging
- buttons
- plastic-covered electrical connecting wire
- plastic curtain wire and eyelets
- draught excluder

Paper

- cardboard tubes/boxes
- milk cartons
- egg cartons
- card/paper, range of thicknesses
- card discs for wheels
- paper lolly sticks

Wood

- wooden beads
- cotton reels
- clothes pegs
- garden canes
- offcuts of wood (from wood-yard, joiners, secondary school)
- lollipop sticks
- dowel

Old toys etc

- old constructional materials
- toys with moving parts
- old toys showing gears, pulleys, levers
- old watches/clocks
- springs, wheels

General

- corks
- wool
- threads
- balloons
- candles

Metal

- pieces of wire
- wire coat hangers
- soft drink cans
- metal rods
- aluminium foil
- aluminium food trays
- nails with large heads
- drawing pins
- paper fasteners
- screws
- nuts and bolts

Sticking

For modelling, you will need sticking, joining and mounting agents.

- Sellotape
- masking tape
- rubber bands

- Marvin Medium glue
- Evostick
- PVA glue

Tools and equipment

Tools and equipment you will need include the following.

- scissors
- glue spreaders
- brushes
- pencils
- rulers
- hole punches

- small hammers
- junior hacksaws
- small pliers
- small work bench with a vice attached, or bench hooks firmly fixed with small G cramps

Many teachers will be very apprehensive at the thought of very young children using the above tools, but if children in the nursery are given tools which they are able to hold with small hands and shown the correct way in which to use these tools, they quickly develop the manipulative skills required to use them with safety. We need to have the confidence to try the tools ourselves and teach the children the simple skills needed to use them safely.

I had the opportunity to observe a group of six children working round a small work bench with some woodwork tools. One little girl was too small to work in comfort at the bench so she stood on a secure wooden box. She tried to hammer the round-headed nails into her piece of wood but found the wood moved around. On the bench there was a small vice which she wound out, and

Left: Look what I've found! *Right:* This will hold the wood steady.

eventually fitted her block into it, tightened it and held the wood securely.

Martin, a 4-year-old, was hammering large-headed nails into a block of wood and ran out of nails. He had lost interest in the activity and was about to leave the bench.

'What is the matter?' I asked him.

'I've used up all my nails!' was his reply.

'Has teacher any more nails?' I asked.

'No,' was his answer as he made towards another activity.

I looked at the hammer which he had been using and realised that it had a claw on the other side of the hammer head.

'Do you know what this is for, Martin?' I asked.

'No,' he replied.

'Let me show you what it will do.'
So back to the bench he came and I pulled out one of the nails he had hammered into his wood. Without a second thought, he took the hammer from me and set about pulling out the nails. He hammered them all back in only to pull them out again, totally absorbed in practising a newly acquired skill.

Materials for older children

Design and technological activities rapidly develop their own momentum, once they are established within the primary curriculum. The children start requesting a more sophisticated range of materials and tools in order to solve more demanding problems.

The following lists are suggestions to enable the more confident teacher to broaden the range of materials available within the classroom along with tips to help with sticking and fastening. (These lists may be more comprehensive than your school will require.)

Timber	Tools	Sticking and fastening
• small sections of various timbers	• hacksaws and other saws	• Marvin Medium
• dowel	• bench hooks	• wood adhesive
• balsa	• glasspaper	• balsa cement
• matchsticks	• hand drills and stands	• masking tape
• lolly sticks	• screwdrivers	• pins and pin pushers
• hardboard, pegboard, plywood, soft insulation board	• pliers	• stapler and staples
	• hammers	• screws
	• files and rat tail	• nails
	• small vice	• glue sticks
	• workmate (adjustable height)	
	• bradawl and glue gun (both teacher tools for safety)	

Paper	Tools	Sticking and fastening
• wide selection of paper and card • maths grid papers of various types • construction straws (jumbo and standard) • newspapers • cardboard boxes and tubes • egg cartons • matchboxes • corrugated cardboard	• stapler • pin pusher • hole punch • scissors	• staples • pins • paper fasteners • paper clips • pipe cleaners • string, cottons • wool • masking tape • Sellotape • wallpaper paste

Plastics	Tools	Sticking and fastening
• ice-cream/margarine tubs • drinking cups • squeezy bottles • drinking straws • plastic tubing of various diameters • guttering • cellophane sheet • foam 'rubber' • styrofoam • coffee jar lids • draught excluder • plastic spoons	• scissors • super snips • hacksaw • glue gun (teacher only)	• clear Bostick • glue sticks

Electrics	Tools	Sticking and fastening
• bulbs and bulb holders • single strand wire • batteries and battery boxes • reed switches • magnets • small electric motors • electrical components from Lego, Construx, etc • pulleys, gears, axles • bacofoil	• wire strippers • small screwdrivers • helping hands device • plastic pipe clips to hold small electric motors and batteries • crocodile clips	• soldering iron, solder and stand (teacher use only) • glue gun (teacher use only) • masking tape

Metals	Tools	Sticking and fastening
• wire and thin rod in a variety of materials, eg brazing rod, florist's wire, electrical wire, chicken wire • drink cans • bottle tops • coat hangers	• wire cutters and strippers • hacksaws • bench hooks • files • tin snips • super snips	• UHU • clear Bostick • nuts and bolts

Clay	Tools	Wheels
• modelling clay • play dough • Plasticine • salt dough • plaster of Paris • Mod Roc • cement • sand • gravel • thermolite blocks	• rolling pin • slip • clay modelling tools • trowel • patterning tools	• wheels from kits • beads • table tennis balls • tin and plastic lids • cheese boxes • cotton bobbins • pipe lagging • card rolls and discs

Fabrics	Tools	Sticking and fastening
• cotton • nylon • patterned materials • hessian • felt • collection of trims • muslin and net	• scissors • sewing machine (when ready) • needles of various sizes • pins	• cottons • varied threads • wools with different textures • glues

Miscellaneous	
• elastic bands • rubber tubing • syringes and plastic pipe clips to hold them in place • pipe lagging • propellers • balloons • springs	• corks • terry clips • cotton reels • clothes pegs • weights • mirrors • PVC adhesive tape • kitchen foil

Storage

It is essential that the materials listed are readily available and stored in such a way that the children can reach them. This is particularly true of 'collectables': if they are sorted and stored tidily, the children can find what they require and they can also be encouraged to bring materials from home and put them directly into their correct storage space. To enable cardboard boxes to be stored more easily, the box joint can be opened to change the box into a flat piece of card. This enables you to store many more in one large box. Children quickly learn that when looking for a suitable box, a small piece of card will make a small box and a large piece a large box. Storing in this way also enables the children to use the opened box in a more versatile way, by putting it together again to make a different shape. Large drums are handy for storing card rolls, smaller items can be collected in plastic margarine containers, plastic sweet jars, etc. Storage does not have to cost money if you make use of 'free', 'throw away' containers.

Some schools have a very limited amount of space, which creates its own problems. Shelves hoarding materials that have been unused for a long time can be cleared, boxes that stack onto each other and fit under a table or work bench, if labelled well, may be a solution. If money is not easily available, you can always look at 'collectable' storage items. The list which follows gives a variety of ideas.

Cheap storage items

- Sectioned bottle boxes (holding 12 bottles) can be used to hold pieces of dowel, wood, etc. Remove the front and cover the box with attractive hessian or wallpaper. Place it on its side, and the items held will be clearly seen and easily available.
- Large tubs can be used for storing wood (those having contained soap powder, dishwasher detergent, etc).
- Use hooks to hold bags, held in place by putting a coat hanger inside – colour coded to help to store relevant materials.
- Shoe storage units provide useful storage space.
- Surplus plastic containers from the chemist (all shapes and sizes)

Ordinary cardboard boxes serve the same purpose as more expensive plastic ones to hold rolls of card and paper.

including film containers) are just right for small items.
- Trolleys are ideal as a mobile resource, sometimes discarded by stores.
- Powder paint plastic buckets (different sizes) with lids.

More expensive items

- Cutlery trays holding Osmoroid jars for small items
- Cat litter trays

Cutlery trays are ideal for separating different kinds of small materials. 'Free' cards rolls are used in this school to hold straws and dowel.

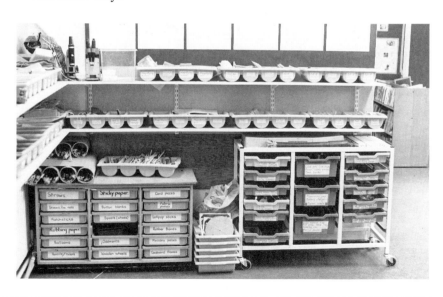

- Shoe tidy boxes
- Corrugated plastic tote boxes
- Stackable Curver boxes
- 'Pel' storage unit with trays (mail order address in list of suppliers)
- Flip-top bin for wood storage
- Caravan-type seating – seats with lids for under-seat storage
- Various technology units are now available, complete with tools (addresses in list of suppliers).

Using available space

One school made use of a corridor in order to store 'collectable' materials. All the classrooms led from one long corridor and it was decided that this was an ideal place to use for storage.

Suitable books to encourage the children in their design-and-make activities were also collected on racks in this area. The storage ideas included brightly coloured, plastic vegetable racks fixed to the corridor wall to hold lids, margarine cartons, yoghurt pots, corks, buttons, beads, bobbins, wheels from old toys, parts from old meccano sets, and all manner of other items which the staff felt would be of use to the children. Parents have now become accustomed to taking their 'collectables' directly to the storage units provided, which saves endless time emptying carrier bags full of items, usually left around the teacher's feet by the children.

Displays

One infant school also decided to use the corridor as storage space but they chose to make this area a permanent display of both natural and man-made materials.

The collection included natural materials such as pebbles, tree roots, stuffed animals, feathers, cones and shells and was extended to broaden the experiences the staff wished the children to have. There were old weighing scales and weights, a hand whisk and a clock with the back removed, so that children

Putting a display where children can see and touch the objects will arouse their curiosity about how things work.

from an early age could begin to develop an awareness of gears and to understand how they worked. Old bottles and books were also on view to help give children the opportunity to develop an understanding of the past.

The fact that the collection was on a corridor meant that all the children passed it as they moved about school. Their natural curiosity led them to stop, look and handle the exhibits and they were encouraged to select items from the shelves and take them to their classroom to sketch, paint, discuss and write about.

These first experiences often led the children into further investigative work. For example:

- Work with construction kits that have gears
- What could they make that needed gears?
- Could they find gears in other objects at school?
- Were gears used in their toys at home?
- Was there a watermill or windmill nearby for a school visit?

The organisation, presentation and wide selection of materials will in itself stimulate the interest of the children. They will be curious to know

- why the materials are there
- how they can be used
- when they are going to be used.

When such curiosity is aroused, the appropriate classroom environment has been set for exciting technological activities to take place.

Part 3   Starting Points

The following sections offer practical starting points for technological activities in the classroom, for children with little previous experience of the subject (whatever their age). Clearly, the way in which you would present some of the activities would vary for older and younger children, but all primary children can benefit from these kinds of experiences. I hope it will be obvious that many of these starting points can arise naturally from what you are already doing.

Two important questions to bear in mind as you begin are:
1 What kinds of design-related experiences has each child had?
2 What skills, concepts, attitudes have these experiences developed? For example:
    – Can the child use a pair of scissors?
    – Can the children co-operate with each other?
    – Do the children understand floating and sinking?

Your observations of the children will enable you to answer these questions. From these observations, you should now be looking at what opportunities you can provide for the children to **use, extend** and **build upon** these experiences.

Where to start

There are many starting points already in existence within the curriculum that can be used to provide a stimulus for technological activities. These include:
• stories, nursery rhymes and poems
• number work
• visits
• news time (show and tell)
• structured play
• topics – themes
• mathematics

- craft – looking at fabrics for collage, designing containers, etc
- science
- music – ideas within songs, work with instruments
- movement
- drama
- computing
- cooking – planning, shopping, making
- co-operative games
- the children's own comments regarding a problem that might arise in or out of the classroom.

In the following sections I have developed some of these ideas in more detail.

5   Story and Rhyme

In this chapter I hope to show how technological activities can arise from the reading of stories. The examples given are stories for very young children but there are numerous suitable stories for older children. Once you've got the general idea, I'm sure you will be able to draw technological activities from stories that you or your children know.

Story is a daily event in the classroom life of young children. Situations in the story, if pointed out by the teacher, can lead easily to children identifying the problems and designing and making their own solutions.

Many stories read to very young children are based around the most familiar place of all – *home*. These stories include: 'The Three Little Pigs', 'Little Red Riding Hood', 'Goldilocks and the Three Bears'. Or what about nursery rhymes such as 'The Old Woman Who Lived in a Shoe', 'There Was a Crooked Man', or 'The House That Jack Built'?

The Three Little Pigs

A class of 5-year-olds in an infant school on the edge of a city were learning about the number three. They had talked about three wheels on their tricycles, three corners on a triangle and the three billy goats in 'The Three Billy Goats Gruff' story. It was this discussion which led to the teacher reading them the story of 'The Three Little Pigs'.

If you look at this story, the first activities you come across are the three different homes that are built (AT 1). The children might first wish to draw or paint pictures of the different homes (AT 2).

Right and opposite: Skills gained by observing and learning from how things work in the world around them are used by these children in their building activity.

These designs could then be built as box models, using construction kits, or using the Wendy house and adapting it to suit the particular section of the story – straw, sticks or bricks (AT 3).

When the children I was observing used the large building bricks to build a home, they could not get the walls to stand up (the bricks were being placed one directly on top of another). In response to the comment 'My bricks keep

falling down!', the teacher took the children outside to look at how the bricks had been used in the building of the school. The children came back to rebuild their house linking the bricks to make a stable structure.

The children also made a child-sized house around one of their classroom desks, using newspaper for the walls and corrugated card for the roof. They painted tile shapes to represent the real tiles on a house. The comments on problems they encountered included: 'The paper goes soggy when we put the paste on it'; 'We shall have to leave it to dry before we can make it any bigger'; 'It isn't very strong and soon tears.'

When the children had finished making their box models, they looked at the materials they had been working with and, using the water tray that was in the classroom, they tested the various materials to see whether they would float or sink.

Below and opposite: The children learned about the properties of different materials from the problems they encountered when building these houses.

Young children, having had such experiences, are usually very happy to talk about how they built their home, what it was made of, the difficulties they encountered and how they might improve it if they had a second attempt (AT 4).

Once the children have been successful in their building, the above example can easily be extended to provide more

opportunities for problem-identifying and problem-solving activities. For example, Were the homes the three pigs made strong? Did they keep the pigs dry if it rained? The children should be motivated to develop more solutions to help the little pigs.

Houses of different materials for the three pigs.

Looking at the programmes of study for Key Stage 1 in *Technology in the National Curriculum*, it is possible to identify the areas that are covered by the problems in 'The Three Little Pigs' story.

Examples of the Implementation of Key Stage 1

I have taken the aspects of the programmes of study for Key stage 1 (from *Technology in the National Curriculum*, March, 1990) which very readily fit the story of the little pigs. This gives some indication of the number of areas covered by the one story and will act as a guide when future work is planned. This breakdown would cover any design-and-make activity, whatever the starting point.

Programme of study	The Three Little Pigs
Developing and using artefacts, systems and environments	
Pupils should be taught to:	
• know that a system is made of related parts which are combined for a purpose;	• the pigs' home
• identify the jobs done by part of a system;	• the door, windows, roof, chimney, floor
• recognise, and make models of, simple structures around them.	• build the pigs' home
Working with materials	
Pupils should be taught to:	
• explore and use a variety of materials to design and make things;	• construction kits, boxes, etc
• recognise that many materials are available and have different characteristics which make them appropriate for different tasks;	• cardboard, wood, straw, paper, clay (for strongest home), plastic (to keep out water), etc
• join materials and components in simple ways;	• cutting and folding paper, sticking card and straw, using paper clips, etc
• use materials and equipment safely.	• safe use of tools
Developing and communicating ideas	
Pupils should be taught to:	
• use imagination, and their own experiences, to generate and explore ideas;	• drawing, painting, modelling and discussing plans for the pigs' house
• represent and develop ideas by drawings, models, talking, writing, working with materials.	• the pigs' house
Satisfying needs and addressing opportunities	
Pupils should be taught to:	
• realise that resources are often limited, and choices must be made;	• selection of materials from available resources with due consideration of the needs of others
• evaluate their finished work against the original intention.	• is the home strong enough for a pig? will it keep out the weather? have the most appropriate materials been used?
In addition, pupils working towards level 1 should be taught to:	
Developing and using artefacts, systems and environments	
• recognise that materials can be linked in various ways to make or allow movement.	• hinges for windows and doors, levers, pivots
Satisfying needs and addressing opportunities	
• talk about what they have done during their designing and making.	• how did they determine the needs of the pigs? how did they build the homes? what materials did they choose and why?

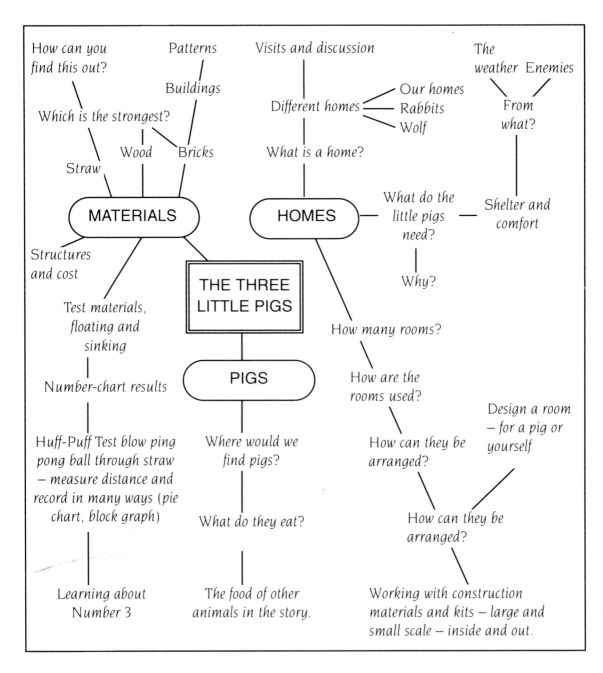

How can you find this out?

Patterns

Visits and discussion

The weather Enemies

Buildings

Different homes — Our homes / Rabbits / Wolf

From what?

Which is the strongest?

Wood   Bricks

What is a home?

Straw

MATERIALS

HOMES

What do the little pigs need? — Shelter and comfort

Structures and cost

THE THREE LITTLE PIGS

Why?

Test materials, floating and sinking

How many rooms?

Number-chart results

PIGS

How are the rooms used?

Design a room – for a pig or yourself

Huff-Puff Test blow ping pong ball through straw – measure distance and record in many ways (pie chart, block graph)

Where would we find pigs?

How can they be arranged?

Learning about Number 3

What do they eat?

How can they be arranged?

The food of other animals in the story.

Working with construction materials and kits – large and small scale – inside and out.

Above is a flow diagram showing some of the work you could develop from this story across the curriculum and some extension ideas. Unfortunately, space does not allow me to include the development of all the written work, maths activities of other areas which could be covered.

Useful materials

Cardboard boxes – all sizes
Card rolls
Straw (grass)
Sticks (lolly sticks)
Bricks (plastic, wood or small home-made from clay)
Plastic straws
Table tennis balls
Paint and crayons
Construction kits – large and small
(Lego, Duplo, Maxi Bricks, NES house bricks, etc)

Other activities

Visit to a building site
Look at dolls house at school and make one using shoe boxes for rooms
Visit castles, caravans, flats, etc
Discuss the homes of the rabbit and wolf and their environment

Number extensions

The number 3
How many animals were there altogether in the story?
Simple graphs – who has the strongest puff?
Measuring and charting on a class graph
Sorting floating and non-floating materials
Patterns in building – Why are they there?
(Science 5/13 series, *Structures and Forces*, Stages 1 and 2, p. 28
– see Bibliography)

Other stories

The Three Billy Goats Gruff
The House That Jack Built
Town Mouse and Country Mouse
Goldilocks and the Three Bears
The Sly Fox and the Red Hen
The Ugly Duckling
The Enormous Turnip
The Enormous Crocodile

Little Red Riding Hood

New words

little	sticks
big	bricks
pig	roof
new	huff
not	puff
bad	blow
wolf	eats
make	hot
straw	splash
house	soup
two	rabbit

Cry for help corner!

Questions for the children:

Can you make the door open?

Can you put windows in for light? Perhaps they could open?

Can a light be put into the house?

Will the roof keep the little pigs dry? If not, what can be used to make it waterproof? (Testing materials) (*Structures and Forces*, p. 32)

Follow-up activities

The number of non-technological follow-up activities that can be developed from such experiences is endless. The following science activity developed directly from the house-building work.

Testing the puff of the children in the class certainly caused great excitement and yet was a most rewarding learning experience. Each child was given a straw and was asked to see how far they could blow a table tennis ball along a straight channel made from large building blocks. The distance the ball moved was then measured and the children made a graph, colouring in the correct number of squares to represent the distance travelled – this showed who had the most puff. When this activity was finished the children asked, 'Why did we use a table tennis ball?' 'Would it be as easy to blow a plastic football or a real tennis ball?' They tried and I'm sure you can imagine the results.

The Flintstones: Fred the Fisherman

Fred Flintstone has a new hobby – fishing. The postman delivers two packages for him (his fishing equipment) and off goes the family on a fishing expedition with unexpected results.

This story provides numerous opportunities for design and technological activities. As the story is read to the children, stops can be made at various stages and questions asked to lead the children's thinking towards problems which arise.

The first sentence is: 'Fred watched from the window as the postman turned into the street where the Flintstones lived.'

Question 1 How does the postman carry his mail? (The children may suggest a bag, trolley, bicycle or van.)

Question 2 Can you design and make a container for the mail?

The questions are worded in such a way that no one solution is hinted at or suggested. When this story was used with teachers and the same technological activities were being identified, one suggestion was, 'Make a Postman Pat vehicle.' This would result in the whole class or group producing identical models, rather than the children identifying the problems and their wide variety of solutions – a basic principle of technology.

The container for the mail might well be a bag made from plastic or fabric, or a vehicle – each fulfilling the postman's need.

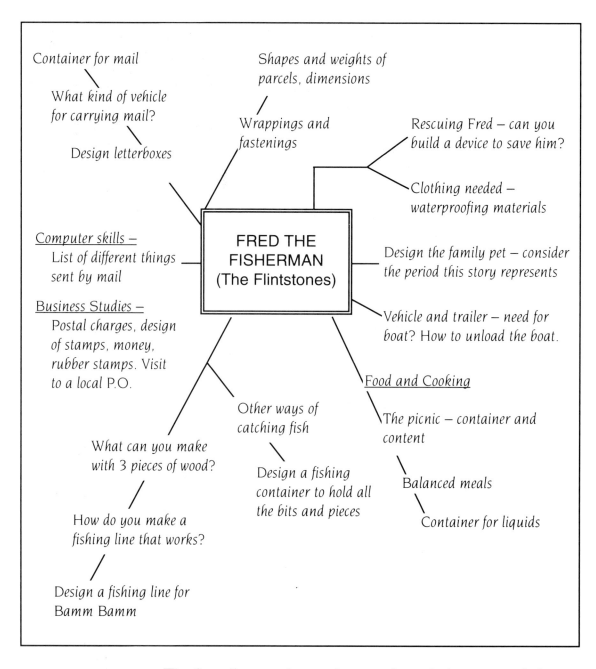

Container for mail

What kind of vehicle
for carrying mail?

Design letterboxes

Shapes and weights of
parcels, dimensions

Wrappings and
fastenings

Rescuing Fred – can you
build a device to save him?

Clothing needed –
waterproofing materials

Computer skills –
List of different things
sent by mail

Business Studies –
Postal charges, design
of stamps, money,
rubber stamps. Visit
to a local P.O.

**FRED THE
FISHERMAN
(The Flintstones)**

Design the family pet – consider
the period this story represents

Vehicle and trailer – need for
boat? How to unload the boat.

Food and Cooking

Other ways of
catching fish

The picnic – container and
content

What can you make
with 3 pieces of wood?

Design a fishing
container to hold all
the bits and pieces

Balanced meals

How do you make a
fishing line that works?

Container for liquids

Design a fishing line for
Bamm Bamm

The flow diagram above takes you through the story and shows
some of the activities which are relevant. They cover the whole
range of areas under the 'Technology' heading, including food,
costings, waterproof fabrics and maths, along with the design-
and-make activities.

Fishing, transportation and designing a prehistoric pet were some of the problems explored in the children's model-making.

Leading the children through the activities with carefully worded, open-ended questions rather than by giving direct instructions, will help them to develop their individual reasoning, thinking and problem-solving skills, so essential in all aspects of their school curriculum.

Technology in nursery rhymes

Some of the earliest verses young children learn are nursery rhymes. Below, I suggest some ideas which can be developed from two familiar rhymes.

Hickory Dickory Dock

How much more exciting 'Hickory Dickory Dock' becomes when opportunities are given to the children to make a clock for themselves and to try to get the mouse to run up and down. Simple materials such as cardboard boxes, straws, lollipop sticks, small garden canes, paper fasteners, cotton bobbins and string can be collected for this work. The children can first look at pictures of many different clocks in books or mail order catalogues. Real clocks can be brought into the classroom and, after discussion, the children can choose a suitable box to make their own clock.

A lovely way to introduce counting to 12 is when the children put the numbers on the clock face. Next come the hands: Are they the same size? Why are they different? What shape can they be? Could it be the first design problem, to cut out a small and large hand for the clock? Where are the hands when the clock strikes one? (The start of understanding how to tell the time.)

The mouse ran up the clock

How can the mouse be made to run up and down? Maybe the children will have lots of suggestions. If not, perhaps the following ideas will be of use to you when they need help.

• If a slit is cut in opposite sides of the box, a cane, lollipop stick or strip of thick card can be pushed through both of the slots. The children can draw a mouse on card and cut it out or make one from wool, material or fur, for example. The mouse can then be glued onto one end of the cane or lollipop stick. If the other end of the cane is lifted up and down the slot, the mouse will run up and down the clock (that is, up and down the side of the cardboard box, the face of the clock being on the front of the box).

- Another idea is to extend the activity on the previous page by using the cane, stick or card as a lever. If you look at the diagrams below, you can see that levers serve two purposes:
  - they can move a large load with little effort
  - they can easily increase movement by altering the position of the pivot.

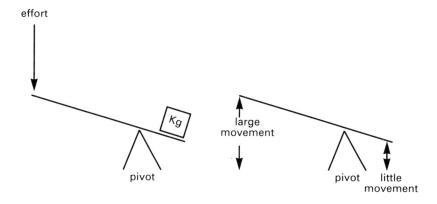

It is to increase movement that the children would want to use a lever on the clock. By fixing the lever onto the box, at the pivot point shown – either inside with the cane, stick or card lever going through the slits, or onto the back of the box – we can achieve a greater distance of movement for the mouse. The lever can be held in place by using a brass paper fastener.
(Both of these ideas will work to move the spider in Miss Muffet.)

- A third way to get the mouse up and down the clock is to make a simple winding device. Or alternatively, the children could design a clock with large hands fitted to an axle. The mouse could be fastened to the axle by a length of string, and as the children turn the hands the mouse will be raised up the clock.

- A further interesting possibility, developing knowledge of

The clock struck one
... by pulling the
pendulum ... the
mouse ran down.

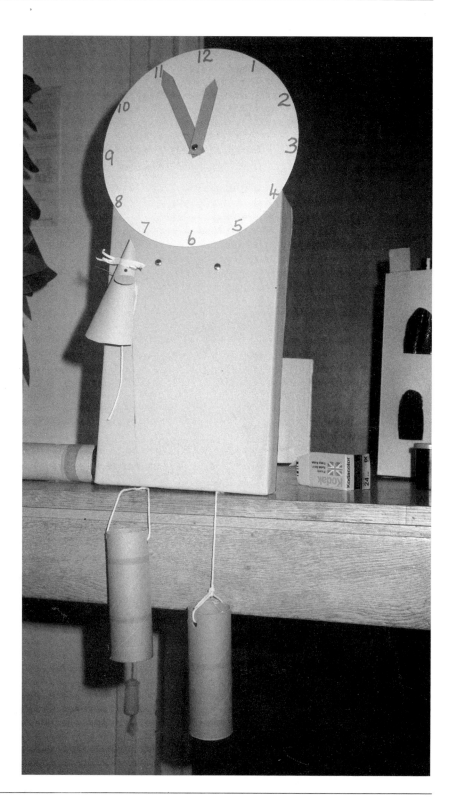

clocks and their mechanisms, is the use of pendulums (toilet roll inners or card rolls are ideal for these). As the children pull one pendulum down, the mouse goes up. Pulling the other pendulum down brings the mouse down again.

These are a few suggestions; the children will wish to try their own versions of these, using materials of their choice. Pop-up books are a good source of ideas for making the kind of movement we have considered for this nursery rhyme.

Jack and Jill

Rather than give suggestions for designing and making activities, the following questions for you to use will encourage children to identify appropriate solutions to the many problems Jack and Jill had to face. It is essential, in approaching this type of work, that you ask open-ended questions, giving the children opportunities to present their own ideas. Try to avoid using words which will influence the children's thinking and indicate the kind of solution you have in mind.

The use of 'collectable' materials together with construction kits will enable the children to design and make a variety of solutions inspired by their responses to your questions. The children may ask other questions which could develop further activities – perhaps leading to rewriting the rhyme to suit today's world.

How can Jack and Jill get the water from the top of the hill to their home?
Is the best solution to collect it in buckets? What other possibilities are there ?
Is the water in a pond or a well? Does this influence the ways in which the water can be collected?
How can you get the water out of the pond or well? (If in a pond, an Egyptian shaduf idea will be helpful; if in a well, a winding device.)
Can the water be channelled in some way so that it runs past their home?

Is it possible for them to live at the top of the hill to save carrying the water?
Is water normally found at the top of a hill? Why not?
How does water reach our homes? (This could lead to testing various materials suitable for carrying water – plastics, metal, etc)
Where does water come from and where is it stored?

There are many stories that can be used as a basis for technological activities. Two other good ideas are the story of Noah's Ark and *Charlie and the Chocolate Factory*. I'm sure you will be able to think of many more.

6   Technology Is Everywhere

Opportunities for technological acivities arise within all areas of the primary curriculum. In this chapter I hope to show, through the case studies described, the wide variety of possibilities available.

Structured play

The following case study aims to show how technological activities can arise from structured play situations.

This was an early technological experience for the teacher so, unsure how to encourage children to identify their own opportunities for technological activities, she structured the first activity herself. She asked her class of 5-year-olds to make something with wheels. The class of 18 split into smaller groups to work with construction kits. One of the groups was using Clever Sticks. They found that when they had built their models, they wouldn't move. The sticks would make rings but the wheels would not go round. They then looked at other construction kits to discover how wheels could be fitted in many different ways so that they would go round.

The children then went out to the school car park to look at different cars. They compared shapes, sizes, colours, makes, etc. Back in the classroom their teacher gave them a selection of old magazines and catalogues. The children found as many pictures of cars as they could and cut out their chosen car shapes. Although their cutting skills were not too precise, this gave them additional practice, and very soon there was a large pile of car shapes to be put into a class book.

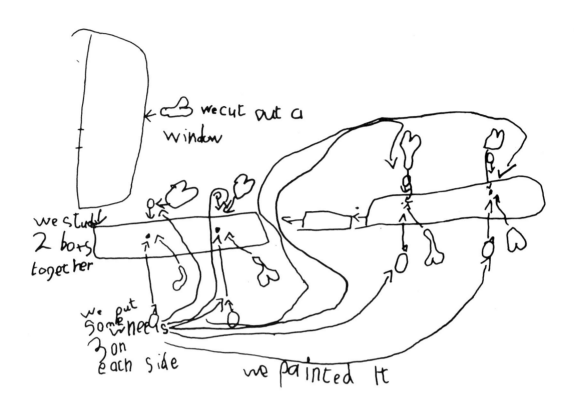

we cut out a window

we stuck 2 boxs together

we put some wheels on each side

we painted it

Jeremy's plan

The teacher suggested that the children look at their own toys to see how the wheels worked on them. The next lesson a number of the children brought their model cars to show the teacher and told the class all about them. The class then drew pictures of these toy models.

Having reached this stage, the teacher suggested they might like to make car box models. As you can imagine, they had a whale of a time choosing the most suitably shaped boxes and deciding on the best way to stick them together. How many wheels did they need? Should they all be the same size? How could they fit them on? Did the vehicle have windows and doors? Was it a racing car or a space machine? Decisions, decisions! Yet the 5-year-olds took all this in their stride and produced the most startling results. When the constructional stage was completed, the children used paint to create the car of their choice.

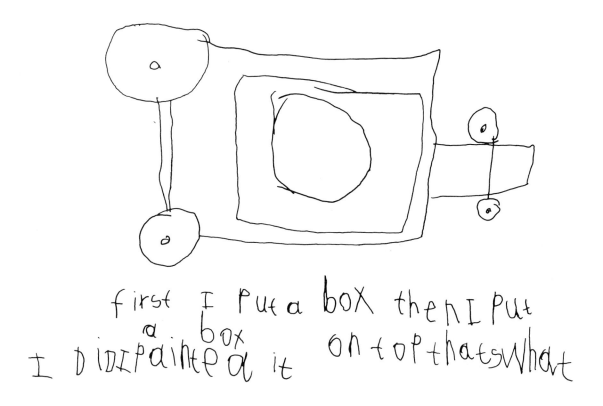

first I put a box then I put
a box
I did I painted it on top thats What

Lucie's plan. When children are motivated by an activity they are very happy to draw and write about what they have done.

The models ranged from a space crane to a red racing car. Out into the playground they went, proudly carrying their vehicles in order to race them across the yard.

The children were very happy to write about their models and draw a picture. Some of this work showed in great detail how the children had set about their task. Jeremy's drawing shows where the cuts with the scissors were made, where the wheels went, and how many boxes were used. If this level of achievement is possible from a child of five, it is exciting to imagine what could be achieved with older children.

Lucie gives a very clear plan of all the pieces she used to make her model and explains how she put the boxes together and painted them.

All this work developed as a result of an opportunity arising during a structured play activity. During the course of solving the problem, the children went through a most varied and relevant learning experience. Such circumstances are ideal for involving young children in design-and-make activities as well as developing their writing, drawing and skills in other curriculum areas.

The classroom in which this work took place with such young children had very limited space for practical activity. The results prove beyond all doubt that it is not the space available which enables such work to take place. Rather it is the teacher who sees and uses the opportunity when it is presented, in whatever form, to broaden the experience of the children in their care.

The child's environment

The 'chit chat' when children first meet their teacher at the beginning of a school day can sometimes lead straight into Technology Attainment Target 1 (see page 11).

Solving a real problem

The morning 'show and tell' session at an infant school on the outskirts of a city was the moment when a real need was identified by a 6-year-old girl. Most of the children lived in high-rise flats and had only one small area in which to play. Some time during the weekend the children's play area near the flats had been vandalised and all the play equipment had been broken.

Alison was very concerned about this when she reported the damage to her class teacher. The teacher fully appreciated the importance of this play area to her children and they had a class discussion about it. Some of the questions and comments from the children were:
'Why should someone want to break our swings?'

'Mummy has nowhere to sit now while we play.'
'The see-saw doesn't work and the roundabout doesn't go round!'

The concern of the children was such that the teacher decided to take them up to the play area to have a look at the damage. The children were very upset and wanted to clear the area of all the broken pieces. This was clearly not safe for small children, so the teacher asked them to tell her how it was arranged before the vandalism.

As they walked back to school they talked about the play area being repaired and what they would like to have if they could choose. They made suggestions and, as this had really fired their interest, the teacher decided to let them make a model of a new play area. The children listed all the items they wished to see there and in several groups set about the task of making the various individual pieces of play equipment.

It was interesting to listen to their ideas – the swings, slides, roundabouts, see-saws were to be replaced, as well as the seats for mums and dads to sit on and wait while they played. Trees were important in their play environment; water and ducks were requested so that the children could watch and feed them but the dangers of water near their play area were explained. The reply from one 6-year-old was, 'We'll have a fence so that water and ducks are on one side and we play on the other but we can still feed them over the fence!' Although this activity took place in 1986, these children were working through most of the Key Stage 1 programmes of study without realising it and before the National Curriculum technology document even came into being!

The children collected their individual playground items together to make their model, using a sand tray as their base. The model included all the things mentioned above plus pipe cleaner people sitting on the seats. A representative from the local recreation department came

The model playground. Even very young children can find solutions to real problems.

to see the finished environment and talked to the children. This resulted in the play area being reconstructed, using some of the children's ideas but, alas, there was no way that the ducks and water could be found a space.

Will the children in this class take greater care of this special area because of their own personal involvement in its design? I'm sure they will watch very carefully and report any misuse or vandalism, as they have helped to recreate a new environment for their own use.

The computer as a starting point with cross-curricular links

Topic work is ideal for teaching technology, as the technological activities which result from the topic will be very relevant to the children. The next case study shows the natural use of the computer as one example of many possible starting points.

The teacher's planned topic for a class of 6-year-old children was 'Movement' but, as the spring term began on a Wednesday, she decided not to start with her planned work until the following Monday. She used the first three days to introduce the children, through the

The children were inspired to make models of Podd.

computer program PODD, to words that expressed movement.

The excitement of the children with the program was such that they took the work along their own path and, though 'Movement' was still the theme, PODD took over and captivated them to such a degree that two months of work evolved. The teacher was taken along by the children and PODD mania ran throughout the class and the school.

Improving keyboard skills came easily with an exciting program like PODD.

Learning about another culture and language was just one of the cross-curricular activities to develop from the topic.

The table on the next pages shows how the work developed and how the National Curriculum in all three core subjects plus technology was covered in a natural development from a starting point which motivated the children. The work was seen by LEA advisors who took examples to an international school in Saudi Arabia to display and discuss at a conference. The advisors brought back items for the children: a guttra (head dress), some stones from the desert and sandalwood perfume. This led the children to find out more about the life and language of children in the Middle East. All this, thanks to PODD.

Title of Topic - PODD

Main curriculum areas - Technology, English, Maths, Science, PE

Suggested content/activity/experience	Skills	National Curriculum ATs
TECHNOLOGY Sorting objects that move/don't move	Sorting Testing	Sci AT 9 Level 1; 10 Level 3a; 6 Level 2a Tech AT 1 Level 1; 3 Level
Using construction kits for model making - models that move in different ways	Planning	Sci AT 10 Levels 1, 2 Tech AT 1 Levels 1, 2, 3; 2 Levels 1, 2, 3a, 3b; 3 Levels 1, 2; 4 Levels 1, 2
Designing boat/raft for pond in Poddland Use of collectables plus wheels, springs to make moveable Podds and Podd vehicles Model of Poddland involving houses, air balloons, Poddmobiles, playground, etc	Problem solving Predicting Working together Raising questions Observation Designing Manipulating materials Working together	Sci AT 10 Levels 1, 2, 3a, 3 Tech AT 1 Level 1; 2 Levels 1, 2, 3d; 3 Levels 1, 2, 3
Badges designed for Podd Club Posters designed for Podd Club pin cushions for Mothers' Day Cards for Mothers' Day Clay plaques of Podd Bubble prints Papier mache Podds Finger puppets Collaborative pictures of Poddland Pictures of Podd using pastel crayons, paints, pencil crayons, felt tips, pencils	Working together Designing Recording in a variety of ways Discussion	These activities cover all Tech ATs 1, 2, 3, 4 Level 1-4 Also Tech AT 5 Levels 1, 2, 3a, 3b, 3c
Cooking – making Podd biscuits and buns	Weighing, mixing	Tech AT 3 Levels 1, 2c; 4 Levels 1a, 3b
Use of Computer	Keyboard skills	Sci AT 11 Level 1; 12 Level Tech AT 5 Levels 1, 2, 3

itudes/ sonal qualities	Organising ideas/words	Key concepts	Evaluation
o-operation		Materials	Much enjoyment Good collaborative work
o-operation erseverance	Pushing, pulling, rolling, springing Directions of movement	Forces Materials	Excellent models produced using Lego, Lasy, Scobar, First Gear
njoyment erseverance	Directions of movements Safety in using tools and glue gun	Materials Forces	Great enthusiam Good models produced Sparked off further ideas for technology – some children brought models they had made at home Science Advisory Teacher an excellent support
espect for thers and for roperty o-operation	Colours, shading, eye-catching designs	Materials	Children enjoyed all aspects of their technology work Imaginative pictures produced of their ideas of Poddland
njoyment o-operation	Safety in using apparatus	Materials	Understanding that misuse of electricity can be dangerous
	Safety in using apparatus	Familiarisation with keyboard	Understanding that misuse of electricity can be dangerous

Title of Topic - PODD

Main curriculum areas - Technology, English, Maths, Science, PE

Suggested content/activity/experience	Skills	National Curriculum ATs
MATHS Sorting objects that move and objects that cannot move	Sorting	Maths AT 10 Level 1a; 12 Level 1
Using Podd worksheets: counting to 5, counting to ten	Numeracy Counting	Maths AT 2 Levels 1a, 1b
More than, less than Simple addition using pictures of Podds	Estimating Understanding number operations	Maths AT 8 Level 1
Using models of Podd and vehicles for preposition work – stating position, on, inside, above, behind, next to	Working together	Maths AT 11 Level 1a
SCIENCE Blowing bubbles – work arising from Podd's whistling tune, 'I'm forever blowing bubbles' Blowing bubbles inside/outside Different methods of blowing bubbles Floating and sinking (objects that float/sink)	Sharing experiences Observation Raising questions	Sci AT 1 Levels 1a, 1b, 2a 2d, 2e; 10 Levels 3a, 3b
PE Children moving about in different ways Moving in different directions	Exploring ways of movement	Sci AT 3 Level 1; 4 Level
Partner work - one being Podd, one being instructor	Working together	

titudes/ rsonal qualities	Organising ideas/words	Key concepts	Evaluation
Developing an enquiring mind	Movement words - rolling, springing	Similarity/ difference Materials	
Perseverance	Names of numbers Symbols of numbers	Addition of numbers 1–10	Children enjoyed using worksheets Other activities needed to stretch the more capable
	More than, less than	Understanding of number Addition of numbers 1–10	
Co-operation Curiosity	On, inside, in front of, behind, next to	Shape and space	Much enjoyment from using models
Co-operation	Floating Blowing air Shape Reflection, colours	Floating/ sinking	
Respect for others	Movement language – running, skipping, hopping, jumping, twisting, curling	Force/energy	Some imaginative movement was developed beside the usual forms of movement
Working together	Backwards, forwards, upwards, downwards, diagonally	Force/energy	Children enjoyed working in pairs

Title of Topic - PODD

Main curriculum areas - Technology, English, Maths, Science, PE

Suggested content/activity/experience	Skills	National Curriculum ATs
ENGLISH Introduction of PODD (computer program)	Keyboard skills Sharing experiences Discussion Social skills	Eng AT 1 Levels 1a, 1c
Discussion about what they think Podd can/cannot do (brainstorming)	Sharing ideas	Eng AT 2 Level 1a
Descriptive writing about Podd	Observation Collaboration	Eng AT 3 Levels 1, 2a
Making list of what Podd can/cannot do	Recording Working together	Eng AT 4 Levels 1a, 1b, 1
Using the computer to check lists	Keyboard skills	Eng AT 4 Level 2a
Using Podd worksheets: pictures, completing sentences, finding words with similar meanings	Recording Observation Discussion Raising questions	Eng AT 5 Levels 1, 2a, 2b 1 Levels 1c, 2c
Writing stories about Podd (adventures of Podd) Using maps/globe to find countries which Podd has visited	Writing skills Working together Reference	Eng AT 3 Levels 1a, 2a, 2 2c, 2d
Setting up of Podd Club: posters, membership cards, badges, rules, passwords	Designing Collaboration	Eng AT 1 Levels 2, 2d; 2 Levels 1a, 2a
Writing names and addresses on Podd membership cards	Writing skills	Eng AT 5 Levels 1, 2a, 2b
IMAGINATIVE PLAY Podd Club house (house/office) Use of telephone directory, timetables, calendar, pens, paper, membership cards, badges, address book, posters	Using different sources of information Sharing experiences	Eng AT 1 Level 1a; 2 Level 1a

titudes/ sonal qualities	Organising ideas/words	Key concepts	Evaluation
Enjoyment Co-operation	Mechanics of using the program Use of space bar and return key Ways of moving	Group identity	Children enjoyed the introduction of the program – good oral contribution about what Podd looked like – many ideas gathered together as a class Children then made lists, had spelling checked and worked together in pairs on the computer Good collaborative work Spelling had to be correct (drawback of program) Good descriptive writing on Podd-shaped paper
	Red, round, tomato-shaped		
Co-operation	Movement words – jump, hop, walk, run Lists	Similarity/ difference	Children enjoyed the worksheets as this approach is not used very often, except with special needs children Words with similar meanings work arose naturally as Podd did the same movements for different words Some excellent adventure stories written – children very keen – now desire to write, though still a few reluctant readers Children very keen about the Podd Club – devised rules and are actively encouraging each other to keep them This topic has been good for the disruptive few, who now seem to be working much better together
Collaboration with others	Words with similar meanings		
Developing an enquiring mind	Countries/towns		
Originality	Rules of living and working together		
	Writing addresses (formal setting out)		
Enjoyment Co-operation	Using telephone directory and timetable in play situation	Imaginative play	Enjoyed by all Different groups seem to arrange area in dirrerent ways – office, rest room, cafe Much language work arose from this activity

Part 4   What the Teacher Should Know

As I have already said elsewhere in this book, the teaching of techniques is not the main purpose of technology. In teaching technology we should be enabling our children to identify problems and opportunities in the real world and to plan, design and make solutions to these problems. The practical techniques are secondary to these basic principles, but are nonetheless essential if children are to design workable solutions to some problems.

There are certain techniques which will be needed time and time again during technological activities and the first chapter in this section describes these techniques and their applications. I hope it will enable you to master these techniques yourself! Obviously, it is up to you to decide when it is appropriate to hold a group or whole-class session to teach them to your children.

The second chapter in this section looks at construction kits – essential tools for technology – and gives you invaluable information on how to choose the right ones for your children.

7   Practical Techniques for Teachers

These techniques are intended to enable you to extend practical experiences when a child's work requires it. It is possible to do this by asking the children open-ended questions rather than by giving specific instructions on how a task should be performed. Children will develop their own ideas and ways to solve problems if you have the courage to stand back and give them the thinking, planning, making and evaluating time necessary. However, you need a certain amount of technical knowledge to pass on to the children as and when needed.

Box modelling

Boxes are obviously 'collectable' materials. In order to make the organisation and use of such 'collectable' materials as easy as possible, a little encouragement of parents may be necessary. If they realise how useful these are going to be for the children, parents can be persuaded to save the various items requested (see the list on page 42) and open the boxes very carefully for further use in school. If parents know where the materials are stored, it is possible that they will sort them into the labelled containers and might even be persuaded to have a rota system for special tidy up sessions! (See Chapter 4.)

The youngest children in a school are very happy to work with cardboard boxes, even more so when they are turned inside out and the writing has disappeared. This means that they have a lovely plain surface on which to paint. The nursery or kindergarten may need help in sticking their opened out boxes back together again but older children could help here or an extra pair of adult hands (parent or auxiliary help?). Using boxes in this way also means that a child is learning that a small piece of card makes a small box (nets in mathematics) and that it is possible to put the box together in a variety of ways. Perhaps it might be possible to decide at this early stage whether doors and windows are needed, as these can be cut out more easily while the box is still flat.

Glue the sides together first. If the box has a glossy surface, rub the joining flap with glasspaper a little so that it will be easier to stick (use Marvin Medium adhesive without adding water – see the list of materials in Chapter 4). If you keep the box flat as you stick the sides, it is easy to press the joint flat on the desk. A strip of masking tape along the joint instead of trying to stick with glue will be easier for younger children – it is possible to paint over the masking tape when the model is completed. Do not stick the two ends as the child may wish to carry things in the box model or adapt it after some work has been done. These ends can always be glued when the model is finished and before painting.

Simple wheels

The first attempts of very young children with boxes may well be just to stick them together, usually as a boat, car or house. Stuck-on lids for wheels may be used, often followed by the statement: 'My wheels don't work!' It is at this stage that other materials could be introduced to encourage the children to try to make the wheels turn on their vehicles.

The materials available to help this to happen could include the following:

• brass paper fasteners with long opening legs
• old knitting needles to use as axles to hold beads
• cotton bobbins, cheese boxes, coffee lids, and other round objects
• lengths of dowel to make axles, 4.5 mm diameter, which fit the cardboard circles of various sizes
• PVC tubing, 5 mm diameter, cut into small pieces to act as washers – to stop the wheel from catching the box and coming off the axle (An aid for cutting straight washers is the round hole for cutting wire on the Plasplug wire strippers.)

Turning a box inside out makes it more suitable for modelling and easier to paint.

Cutting wheel spacers
and axles with
Plasplug

Children might first try pushing the axle straight through the box but will have problems getting it through straight – usually not all the wheels touch the floor doing it this way. Centimetre-squared paper stuck on the box and counting the squares up and across might be one solution, but the children will surprise you with their own.

Turning a hole punch upside down enables you to see exactly where to make the hole in axle holders.

The axles can be attached by making axle holders, using four equally sized strips of thick card with a hole punched in each. The hole is made by using a single or twin hole punch, turning the hole punch upside down without its plastic base so that you can see your pencil mark for the hole, or by using a plier-type punch (such as is used for leather).

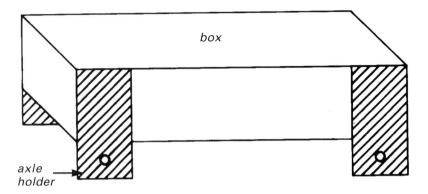

The axle holders are then stuck to the sides of the box so that the axle (dowel) can go through the holes under the box. Make sure that the dowel is cut long enough to hold whatever you are using for wheels and spacers. If the wheels rub against the card, cut short lengths of plastic tubing (see materials list) to help the wheels to move more freely. These can also be used on the outside of the wheel to stop it falling off the dowel.

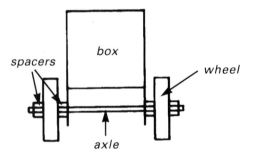

Materials for use as wheels

Searching through the 'collectable' materials with the children, for ideas for making wheels, will encourage them to look for round shapes and help them to identify suitable items. These can be stored together to help very young children but very quickly the children will select other types of material for larger wheels, fatter wheels, etc.

Coffee jar lids, cheese boxes, bobbins, paper plates, toilet roll and kitchen roll inners are all possibilities for collectable materials.

- Inside a round coffee jar lid there is a card circle which can be used for one kind of wheel while the plastic lid will make another. It may be necessary to drill a hole in the plastic lid, the centre is marked if you look very carefully, or you could use a bought card circle to find it. On its own the lid will wobble on the axle but if it is strengthened with 8 mm square wood, as shown below, it will make a good, strong wheel. The outer edge is ridged which will help it to grip on a variety of surfaces.

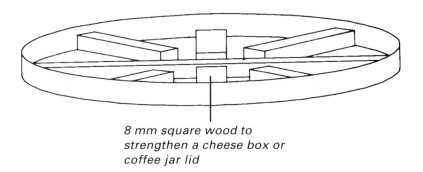

8 mm square wood to strengthen a cheese box or coffee jar lid

Once the wood has been stuck onto the plastic (across the centre and in the shape of a hot cross bun) and the glue has set, the lid can be drilled to take the dowel. Using spacers, as shown above, will hold the lid away from the box.

- Cheese boxes make good wheels; they are a suitable size for young children and can be strengthened by sticking wood in the centre before drilling a hole, this will enable the wheel to stay upright on the axle and not flop from side to side.

- If paper plates are stuck back to back, the children will have large wheels which are quick to make for larger constructions.

- Cotton reels covered with pipe lagging make quick, effective wheels. The hole in the cotton reel may need a small piece of 5 mm tubing inside to fix the reel firmly onto the axle. The drawing shows an easy way to measure the pipe lagging, which can be cut by using a hacksaw.

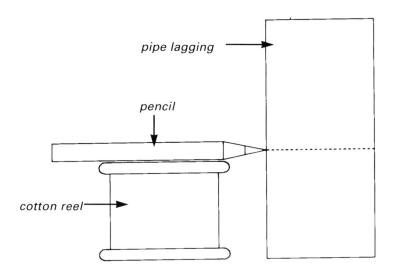

pipe lagging

pencil

cotton reel

Ready-made wheels

It is now possible to purchase a variety of wooden and plastic wheels and axles as well as Lego ones. These are easy to use but very expensive if you wish all the children to work in this way, taking their prized models home when they are finished. It might be helpful to have some bought wheels available so that the children can get their model moving very quickly. This should lead them to making their own wheels in as many ways as possible. Ready-cut cardboard discs in various sizes, with a hole in the centre to take the axle, can now be bought. These save a lot of time in cutting out circles (usually the teacher's task as the children are unlikely to have yet developed the manipulative skills of using scissors so accurately). If card discs are used on their own, they are quite fragile and bend very easily but by sticking several of them together it is easy to obtain a stronger wheel.

A useful teacher tool for larger circles is the Olfa circle cutter. This proves very successful after a little practice and will cut through quite thick card. It is like a pair of compasses but, instead of having a pencil, there is a small blade which cuts out the circle. The art of using the cutter is to place the card to be cut on an old magazine or pile of newspapers. Place the Olfa circle cutter on the card and move the card steadily round so that the blade cuts through it. (This takes a little while; do not try to cut a circle in one turn of the card.)

To make the bought cardboard discs more substantial, the drawings below give a number of ideas, using simple materials:
- Foam pipe lagging of various sizes
- Toilet roll and kitchen roll inners
- Corrugated card
- 8 mm square wood section
- Lollipop sticks

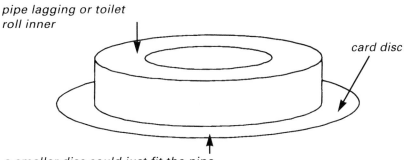

pipe lagging or toilet roll inner

card disc

a smaller disc could just fit the pipe lagging, which would then act as a tyre

another card disc is stuck on top, then the wheel is drilled in the centre to take the dowel axle

8 mm square wood for strength

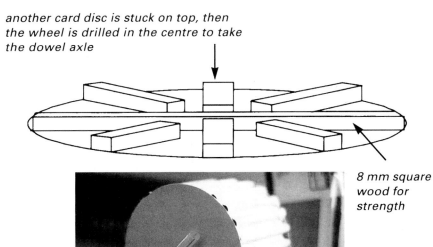

Using corrugated card is one way of strengthening wheels made of card circles.

Toilet roll inners are not very strong but can be reinforced by sticking two together. Split one of them lengthways, spread the outside with glue and slot it inside another roll. Leave this overnight to dry and then it is possible to cut it into thin strips to use sandwiched between card discs. If the same-sized discs are used as the diameter of the tube, you have a wheel. If larger card discs are stuck to the roll strip, it has made a very useful pulley.

Using card rolls

Children often like to use a card roll in their box modelling. If this is to be used as a tower (lighthouse or centre of a roundabout) and needs to turn, it is hard to find a method which holds the tube stable and yet allows movement. One idea is to make a hole for the roll in the top of the box and wedge a slightly wider roll inside, glued to the base. The tall roll will then fit through the hole in the top and be supported by and turn within the larger roll inside the box.

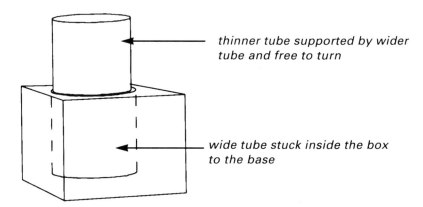

thinner tube supported by wider tube and free to turn

wide tube stuck inside the box to the base

Often, a length of dowel is required to be supported as part of a box model. This can be placed through the box and held securely in a cotton reel stuck to the base of the box.

Children will probably wish to glue many boxes together to achieve their car, caravan, train or whatever. When all the sticking and fastening on of wheels has been achieved, the box model can be decorated. Some children may just wish to paint

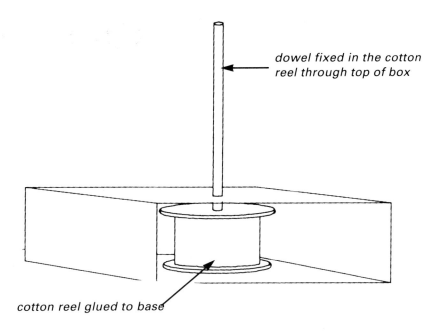

dowel fixed in the cotton reel through top of box

cotton reel glued to base

while others will use clear materials for windows, add bumper bars, mudguards, etc. The degree of involvement depends on the child and the time available but it is essential that children are able to complete the work to their satisfaction. A sketch or painting of the finished work is often very willingly produced along with a brief description of the model and its construction.

Classroom discussion regarding how many different objects have been used for wheels, how successfully they work when tested, and so on, will help to broaden and develop children's use of materials and help them to improve future models. A folder would be helpful in which to save their drawings, paintings and written descriptions. These will form the basis for your assessment of the child's experience and stages of development and will also help the next teacher with progression.

More moving parts

So far, only wheels and rolls have been turning. What other movement is possible with simple box construction techniques?

Turntables for fire engines, cranes, etc

- A paper fastener joining two boxes will enable the top box to turn.

- Two coffee jar lids, one slightly larger than the other, the smaller one containing beads, marbles or ball bearings, the other lid placed over the top so that it moves easily. The large lid is then stuck under the top box, the small one stuck on top of the bottom box, then the two are put together.

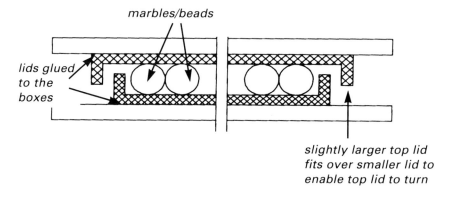

marbles/beads

lids glued to the boxes

slightly larger top lid fits over smaller lid to enable top lid to turn

Extending skills: more rigid materials

Children who have developed their box modelling skills, and have become accustomed to solving simple problems with 'collectable' materials, will quickly find these materials frustrating and limiting in their possibilities.

The point at which this stage is reached depends on the experience of the child, not on their age. Some children may be ready for a wider variety of materials at the age of six while others may not broaden their materials until the age of eight. It is important to remember that, though the National Curriculum documents refer to age bands (Key Stage 1, 5–7 years, Key Stage 2, 7–11 years), we must be concerned with the stages of development rather than the age of the child concerned. As technology is new to most children, they may all be at the same starting point, the older children moving more quickly through the levels than the younger ones. We do not give young children Shakespeare to read before they have basic reading skills! We must avoid similar, inappropriate tasks as we plan our work in technology.

Working with wood

Many children are now familiar with a simple wood and cardboard technique (developed by David Jinks, Senior Lecturer at Bishop Grosseteste College, Lincoln) which, once mastered, gives them wider opportunities to build strong, lasting models which will move with more accuracy. (This technique is described in more detail on the next pages.) The children will be introduced, when ready, to the small range of simple materials, tools and equipment listed on pages 45–7.

It is essential that young children are shown how to handle a junior hacksaw safely. Although this saw is really intended to cut metal, the blade having very small teeth, it is an ideal size for small hands and is safe if used with care. It is never possible to remove danger completely from the classroom environment but other items we use – scissors, pencils, compasses, for example – can be equally, if not more dangerous if they are not handled with safety in mind. The bench hook is a device intended to help the child to hold small sections of wood firmly while they are using the junior hacksaw and is there to protect the desk from any possible damage. This means that sawing can take place in the classroom and does not require a special work area such as a craft room.

Opposite: Children
can use woodwork
tools quite safely
when taught the
correct technique.

Making a chassis

To help develop manipulative skills along with technological
activities, the simplest wooden frame for the children to make is
the chassis. This is the name given to a rectangular frame onto
which wheels are attached using axle holders.

An ideal way to start teaching the skills is to work with a small
group of perhaps six children. First, show them how to hold the
wood on the bench hook, which offers a cutting edge for both
right- and left-handed children. If you encourage them to put
the effort into holding the wood still and firm rather than
pressing on the saw, they will let the teeth do the work of cutting
through the wood. To make the rectangular shape for the
chassis, two long pieces and two small pieces are needed. Once
the measurements of these have been decided, the children can
measure one of the long pieces, cut it and use that piece of
wood as the pattern for the second. They can repeat this
procedure for the small pieces.

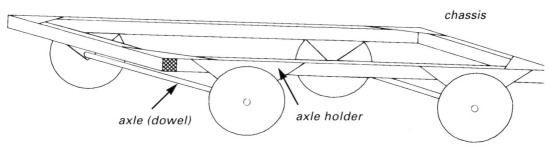

chassis

axle (dowel)   axle holder

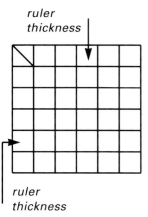

ruler
thickness

ruler
thickness

The traditional way of joining wood together is by using nails or
screws but young children often find these methods very
disappointing as the wood tends to split and not hold successfully.
It is possible to use thin card triangles and PVA to join the corners
of the wooden frame. The children can make the triangles from a
piece of thin card (230 microns) using their ruler thickness to draw
parallel lines. They can then turn their card round and draw
parallel lines again so that they have a sheet of squares.

With young children, perhaps one child could hold the ruler (the
widest possible) tightly while the other child draws the pencil lines.

Once these squares have been drawn, the children can cut them out and by cutting across the diagonal produce a right-angled triangle. It is not so important if the diagonal line is not cut perfectly straight. The important part of this triangle is the right angle, which helps the children to join the wood carefully to make a right-angled corner with their wood and an accurate rectangular frame. This cardboard triangle hides the slight inaccuracies that are inevitable when using a hacksaw for the first time.

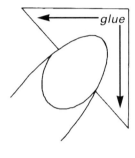

If the children hold the triangle with their thumb in the middle of the longest side and paste round their thumb, they put the glue just where it is needed to stick onto the wood and do not make a mess on the table.

To make life as easy as possible, keep the PVA in small film containers (free from film processing firms), filling them only half full. If you encourage the children to put their spreader on the lid when they are not using it, this saves a mess on the table top and the container doesn't fall over. (Lollipop sticks make good spreaders and are inexpensive.) If the lid is replaced when it is not in use, the glue is kept in good condition until it is needed again. (No more throwing away of yoghurt pots full of dried-up glue on Monday mornings, before the head sees them!)

The thin card triangles are stuck on one side of the frame first, then the frame is turned over and the process is repeated on the other side, making a sandwich of wood between card. This frame then needs to dry.

While the frame is drying, the children can make thick card triangles (card of 750 microns) to use as axle holders. The squares are drawn in just the same way as for the corners but instead of cutting single squares, the children need a block of four squares. They should then draw two lines from corner to corner.

cutting axle holders

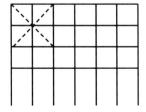

If they cut along the dotted lines as shown, left, they will have triangles which are twice the size of the thin corner ones they have been using to build the frame.

To find a suitable place to punch a hole for the axle to go

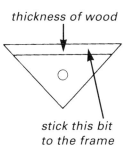

thickness of wood

*stick this bit
to the frame*

through, hold the triangle against the strip of wood and make a line which shows where the glue is needed to stick it onto the frame. Halfway between the point of the triangle and this line, put a dot. If you turn the hole punch over and take off the plastic container that holds the bits, you can put the triangle into the hole punch and see the dot you have made. Punch the hole and use this as a pattern for the other three axle holders, so that the hole is in the same place on each axle holder.

The axle holders are now ready to stick onto the wooden frame. It is very important that they are fixed accurately opposite each other – a tip is to slot a length of dowel through the axle holders while the glue is still wet to give you a line to check against the frame.

If a particular-sized frame is required, for the children to fair test the performance of their finished chassis, much discussion can be encouraged to enable them to find a way of measuring the 8 mm square section wood so that their finished shape is 20 x 7 cm.

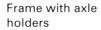

Frame with axle
holders

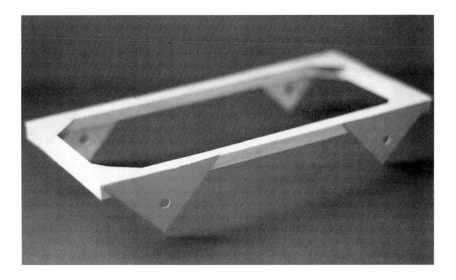

The following points need to be considered: ·

- Do we ask young children to measure in millimetres?
- How can they achieve the accurately sized frame?

The discussion will usually bring up the suggestion that the first piece to measure is 7 cm and that this can be cut and used as the pattern for the other piece.

How can the longer pieces be measured?

The children will suggest that the length is 20 cm, forgetting the thickness of the short pieces of wood at each end. When this is pointed out, they will measure 20 cm, put the two 7 cm pieces already cut next to the 20 cm pencil mark, mark off the two thicknesses of wood, and cut the shorter length as shown in the drawing. They can then use this piece as a pattern for the second piece.

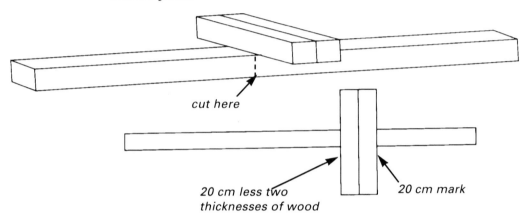

cut here

20 cm less two
thicknesses of wood

20 cm mark

Does it make any difference which way the frame is built?

Maybe it does if the chassis is going to be powered in some way.

Is one way of building it stronger than the other?
How can it be powered?

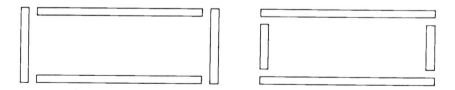

Does it make any difference which way the frame is built?

(Pages 113–23 will give you some ideas for powering the children's models.)

Wheels

There are many ways of making wheels (see pages 96–100) if bought wooden wheels prove to be too expensive. The manufactured card discs with a hole punched in the centre save all the trouble and time needed to draw and cut out circles. (Olfa circle cutters are a useful teacher tool for larger circles, see page 98.) The discs on their own are not very strong; stuck together in threes they make a possible thin wheel but if stronger wheels are required perhaps some of the earlier ideas will be useful.

Tyres

If the card discs, when constructed into wheels, do not grip the floor, carpet or table very well, various forms of tyres can be tested. Open a length of masking tape out and roll the finished wheel along the centre of the strip. It sticks as it rolls, which is easier than cutting a length from the roll first. When the tape has gone all the way round, cut it from the roll and snip round the edges so that they can be stuck down flat.

When powering a chassis, some wheel spin can occur. Materials to use as tyres are rubber bands, corrugated card, draught excluder, pipe lagging and strips of balloons. A balloon with both ends cut off and sliced in two will make two lovely, colourful tyres and stay on firmly. Children can save damaged balloons to use in this way.

Rollers

In order to use a syrup tin as a roller, a hole has to be made in the base and the lid. It is possible to find the centre by placing one of the manufactured card circles on the base and marking through the centre hole. A strip of masking tape on the tin will enable you to see the mark clearly. Hold the can upright on a work bench or classroom table (the strongest part on the table is directly over a leg), place a centre punch on the pencil mark and tap with a hammer. Turn the punch after each tap. The centre punch pushes the sharp edges of the hole inside the can. *Never* drill metal. If the hole in the can is too big, a card disc can be

Using rollers (in this case, a custard powder tin) in model making.

stuck over the hole with a glue gun. Weight can be added to the tin by filling it with sand or pebbles.

A length of kitchen roll, whisky bottle holder, tennis ball container or carpet roll will also make an excellent roller. The ends of the roll can be covered by using the appropriately sized card disc.

Another three-dimensional shape: the cuboid

Older junior children need additional skills to develop their technological capability.

If a class of children are taken to observe a building site, they return to school full of excitement and with lots of ideas about objects (artefacts) they have seen and would like to make. These include the buildings, cranes, lorries, dumper trucks and so on. To develop these ideas they need skills that enable them to move from the flat wooden frame to the cuboid or other three-dimensional shape. Children may find it helpful when building these new shapes, to work above squared paper – this helps them to be accurate.

To make a cuboid, it is easiest to make the two largest rectangles first. When the two shapes are made, place one on top of the other and move it around to find the most accurate fit. Now mark them – this will help when the uprights are fitted. Cut eight of the larger triangles, fold down the centre and glue round the corners of the square frames.

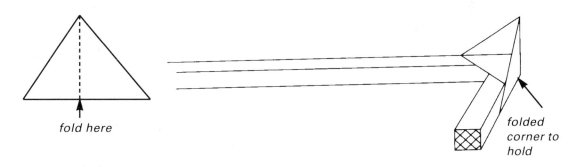

fold here

folded corner to hold

Stick the double-sized, folded card corners to the two rectangles before putting the four uprights in place.

The top frame should fit neatly over the uprights.

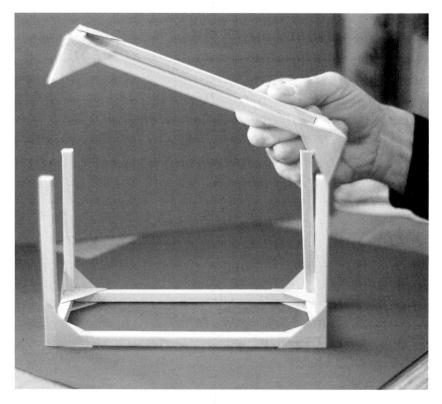

The basic cuboid can be added to and adapted for all sorts of models

Allow a short time for these corners to dry before sticking the uprights into the double corners of one of the rectangles. Wait a while for these to set before gluing the other corners on the second rectangle. Lift this over the top and carefully press the uprights into position.

Once the children are confident with this method of construction, they are able to adapt it to suit any shape they require in their problem-solving activities.

Powering the models

Using air as a source of energy

Balloons can be used to make things lift – tip-up trucks, bridges, flowers growing out of card tubes, rabbits popping out of hats, jack-in-the-boxes, egg box mouths opening.

The balloon is fastened with masking tape or a rubber band onto PVC tubing 5 mm in diameter. The other end of the tubing is either blown by mouth or taped onto a squeezy bottle used as a pump. Another excellent way to secure a balloon is to put the balloon neck over a thin cotton reel, the hole in the other end just fits the 5 mm plastic tubing. Each child could have their own piece of tubing and put it into the cotton bobbins on other models to test. This would avoid children blowing down each other's piece of tubing.

It is possible to make a simple pop-up toy by using two card tubes of slightly different diameters, one sliding easily within the other. If a top (Father Christmas, flowers, rabbit, rocket) is designed for the thinner tube and the base is covered with a card disc, a balloon placed inside the larger tube under the thin tube, will have a flat surface against which to push when inflated, and the air will lift the rabbit or flower above the level of the outer tube. Plastic bottles with the tops cut off can be used as an alternative to card tubes.

The space the balloon is in has to be restricted to achieve

as the balloon is inflated, the flower pot or Father Christmas will move up

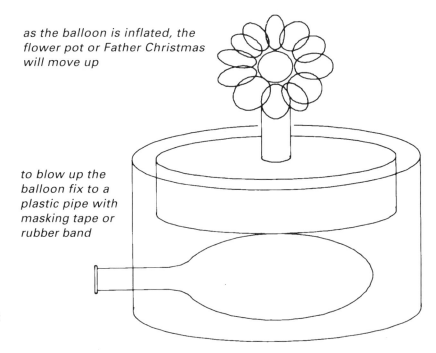

to blow up the balloon fix to a plastic pipe with masking tape or rubber band

The dragon's head rises when the balloon inside its body is inflated so that it presses against the bottom of the lever.

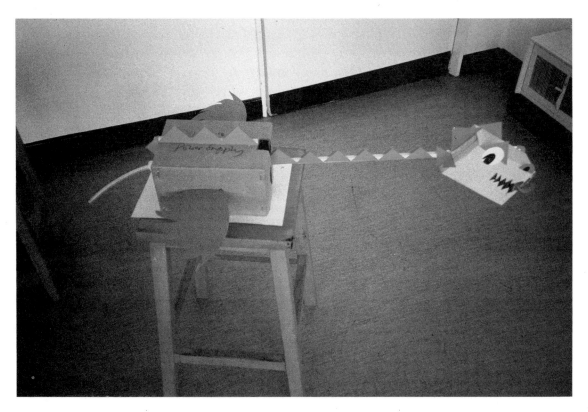

maximum lift. Additional lift can be obtained if the balloon, when inflated, presses a lever.

Plastic lemonade bottles make ideal towers for bridges. If a balloon is fitted into the top of the bottle, its movement is restricted, forcing it downwards when inflated. This pushes the balloon against the arm of the bridge, thus raising the bridge. As the air is released, the bridge is lowered. Using clear plastic bottles, the children can see what is happening to the balloon as it is filled with air.

as the balloon inflates, the air pushes down on the wooden arm and the bridge rises

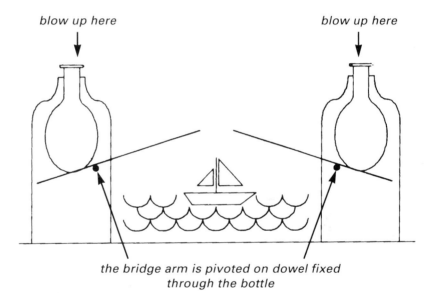

blow up here　　　　　　　　　　　　　　*blow up here*

the bridge arm is pivoted on dowel fixed through the bottle

Extension ideas with balloons

So far, the examples given have all been of lifting mechanisms. Air can also make things move horizontally. The following questions will help you to extend work in this area with older children.

Will the air stored in a balloon move a chassis (the base of a vehicle – see page 105) or model animal across the floor? What is the easiest shape to move using air – a rectangle or triangle? How can you find this out?

How will you fix the balloon to the shape you wish to move? (A card disc with the balloon through the centre hole can be attached, but watch the size of the centre hole. A cotton bobbin, slim shape, is ideal.)

Which size of wheels makes the shape move as far as possible? (Large, thin and light rather than small, thick and heavy!)

If the best shape is triangular, how can the wheels be attached?

Is a long balloon more effective than a round one?

Does the balloon rest on the shape, causing drag? Can a support be added to eliminate this?

Does more than one balloon on the same shape make any difference? (Side by side or one inside the other.)

These are some examples of simple ways for young children to explore how things work and how they can make things that move. By giving children the opportunities to work in this way and to use manufactured construction kits and toys, you are stimulating their curiosity, imagination and inquisitiveness and helping them to understand and develop an awareness of how machines, equipment and toys in the real world work. You can link these activities with examples of real life situations; for example, an air bag is placed under a crashed car and air is blown into it to lift the vehicle. A similar idea is used in hospitals to lift damaged limbs with minimal pain. One of the latest uses is inside a car. If the car is involved in an accident where the impact is at the front of the vehicle, a bag automatically inflates between the screen and the passengers which stops them from being thrown forwards and averts serious injuries.

Powering a chassis

If your children have made chassis following the instructions on pages 105–108, they will each have one of the same size, made from the same materials and with the same-sized wheels (made by strengthening card discs with lollipop sticks). The next step is to give them all a drawing pin and a rubber band of a standard size (thin, medium-sized).

Can they use the energy stored in the rubber band to power their chassis? (A tip to help the teacher – hook the band over the drawing pin, which is fixed into the centre of the front of the chassis, wind the other end of the band round the axle as tightly as possible. Test the result!)

These are some of the ways in which a group of children can investigate the performance of their standard 20 cm x 7 cm chassis and record their fair testings in various ways.

How does it travel on different surfaces?
How does it travel up different gradients?
How is the distance travelled affected by
    – changing the number of turns of the band?
    – testing with one band, two bands?
    – testing with various thicknesses of rubber band?
    – driving from the front axle?
    – driving from the back axle?
    – testing on a fixed axle?
    – testing on a free axle?
How can it be made to move a fixed distance?
How can different weights be carried over a fixed distance?
What is the maximum weight that can be carried up a fixed
    gradient?
How is performance affected by
    – the thickness and weight of wheels?
    – the size of wheels?
    – different construction of wheels?
Timing over a fixed distance.

Can the children think of any other testing which they could do?

How many different ways can they think of to record their results?

So far, only flat, rigid shapes have been described, but after children have tested their chassis, they may wish to look at more aerodynamic shapes (triangular chassis). Triangle-shaped pieces of card do not have to be used for joining more awkward corners. Any strip of card will stick across the join and the excess card will trim off easily when the glue has dried.

A triangular chassis can be made with three wheels.

Powering a triangular chassis

Another way of powering a chassis is with a balloon. After constructing a triangular chassis, it is important that the holder for the balloon is fixed very securely onto the chassis. The holder can be a card disc, a thick piece of card with a hole, a cotton reel with suitable hole, the top of a washing up liquid bottle (the hole requires careful enlarging to give maximum effect) or a piece of plastic tubing. The children will need to experiment with the aperture to achieve the best performance. Ensure that the balloon is blown up fully and remember that when balloons are continuously inflated, they lose their elasticity.

What other ways can children find to power the chassis? (They could adapt them as land yachts, looking at different kinds of sails. A hairdryer or cylinder vacuum cleaner could be used for power.)

Pneumatics and hydraulics

A natural progression, after children have used balloons as a lifting device, is to look at pneumatics. This word looks daunting but simply means a system using air as a source of energy. One kind of pneumatic system requires two syringes and a length of 3 mm plastic tubing. It is important, when working with children using syringes, for them:

• to identify the use of hydraulics and pneumatics in real life. Visits to building sites and shopping precincts, watching vehicles pass school are all possible sources for identifying real life applications linking with their classroom work
• to be told very clearly that the only syringes they use come in sealed packages. They must be told of the dangers of touching other syringes found on the beach, in parks, and other public places.

The syringes you can buy are manufactured for medical injections, not for engineering activities. You can, however, use two 10 mm syringes to mechanise simple devices.

A system filled with air is not as efficient as one filled with water (hydraulics) as air can be compressed where a liquid cannot. (The air is bled out of car brake pipes to leave just the liquid for maximum efficiency.) Children need to work with the syringes filled with air first, to appreciate the difference when they fill them with water.

Filling the system

The aim, when filling the system with water, is to ensure that there are no air bubbles trapped inside. You can do this by placing the whole system under water, but filling in this way causes a lot of water around the classroom!

The easiest way is to fit the two syringes on to the 3 mm tubing – if both plungers are in and you try to pull them out you will find that you have a vacuum.

Take both the plungers out and then replace them and the system will be filled with air.

To fill it with water, take both plungers out of the syringe bodies, fill one of the syringes with water and hold it high so that the water finds its own level and fills the lower syringe.

When the lower syringe is completely full, put the plunger in and press down to the bottom. (This sends all the air through the tube and out of the top syringe.)

Then top up the higher syringe with water and put in the plunger.

You will find that this system is then free of air bubbles and not too much mess has been made.

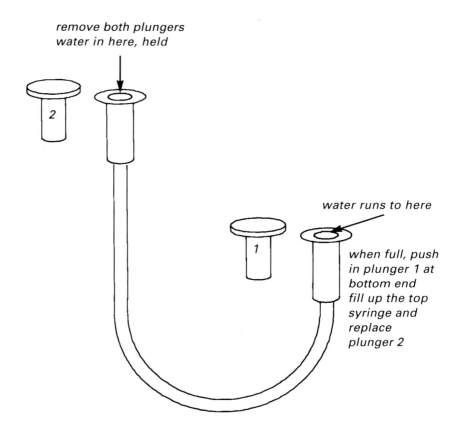

remove both plungers
water in here, held

water runs to here

when full, push in plunger 1 at bottom end fill up the top syringe and replace plunger 2

Fixing the syringe in place

In most models, at least one syringe needs to be fixed securely within the model.

The syringes fit well into 15 mm plastic pipe clips. However, as these clips are a little tight, it is necessary to put them into hot water for a short time to make the plastic more pliable. Always press the syringe into the clip at either the open end or the base of the syringe (where it is strongest) as it is easy to split the syringe if it is pressed into the clip in the middle.

The pipe clip can be fixed in place by using a 3/4 inch cross-head wood screw. The 8 mm wood is not wide enough to hold the pipe, so use a double thickness – two pieces of 8 mm glued together and left to dry or a piece of 19 mm x 8 mm, which can now be purchased. The clip will also fix by using hot glue. If these methods of fixing are not possible for small fingers, masking tape will hold the body of the syringe or it can be slipped into a piece of pipe lagging which can be taped on to or wedged inside the model.

All the above methods of fixing are to hold a syringe rigid. There are occasions when the fixing needs to be flexible and this can be achieved by attaching the plunger to the object to be moved by means of a rubber band so that some curve in the movement can be achieved. (You could use this, for example, to push round a gear fixed to the base of a crane in order to move the crane round.)

Uses for hydraulics

A hydraulic system can be used to activate levers, to lift, lower and to turn. It is important to remember that the object being moved will only move as far as the length of the plunger. This movement can be increased by using a lever.

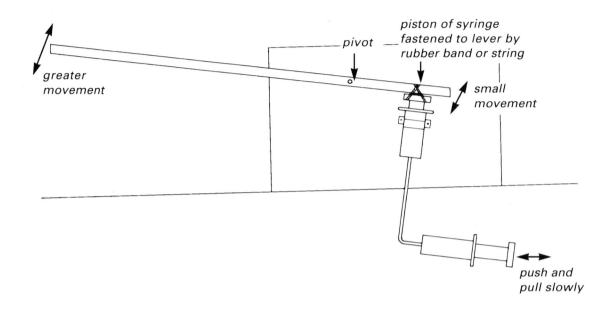

pivot

*piston of syringe
fastened to lever by
rubber band or string*

*greater
movement*

*small
movement*

*push and
pull slowly*

Horizontal movement – to open or close a match box or other drawer action model. If you turn this on its end you have a lift shaft or cage in a mine. The plunger is attached to the drawer of the box.

*drawer action
can be turned into a mine cage or lift if held upright*

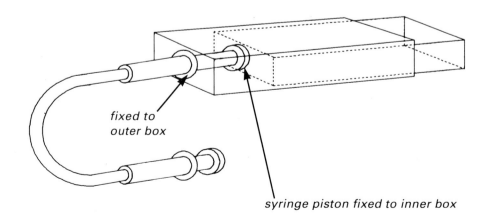

*fixed to
outer box*

syringe piston fixed to inner box

Vertical movement – jack-in-the-box or pop-up toy, dentist chair.

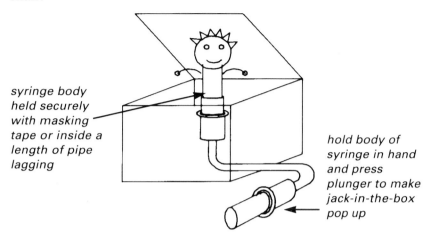

syringe body held securely with masking tape or inside a length of pipe lagging

hold body of syringe in hand and press plunger to make jack-in-the-box pop up

Other uses – a tip-up lorry, fireman's ladder, fork lift truck, weather house, opening and closing of lift doors.

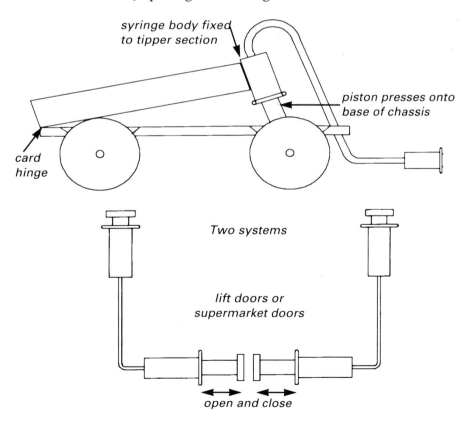

syringe body fixed to tipper section

piston presses onto base of chassis

card hinge

Two systems

lift doors or supermarket doors

open and close

Ideas for making gears

Gears can be used in a variety of ways – as lifting devices, windmills, waterwheels, etc. Gears are used to change the direction of movement or to speed up and slow down movement.

Equal gears to change the direction of movement

Draw a plan of two hexagons on a sheet of paper.

Place a cardboard disc over one hexagon, but so that it is still visible, and secure it carefully with two small strips of masking tape.

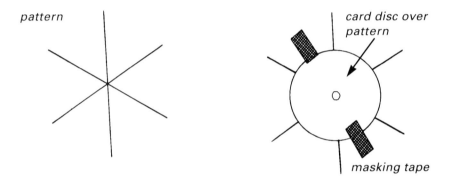

pattern

card disc over pattern

masking tape

Glue a matchstick to the card circle, not to the plan, but lining the matchstick between the hole in the centre of the disc and one of the corners of the hexagon. The end of the stick should just touch the hole in the card and not cover it.

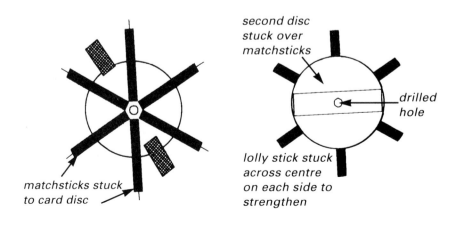

second disc stuck over matchsticks

drilled hole

matchsticks stuck to card disc

lolly stick stuck across centre on each side to strengthen

Glue on six matchsticks in this way and cover them with another card disc. Cut two lengths of lollipop stick the diameter of the card disc and glue across the centre of the discs, one on each side. This strengthens the gear.

This gear needs to be left under a weight to dry overnight if possible. Using the second hexagon, make a second gear in the same way.

When dry, drill tight-fitting holes in the centre and put a length of dowel through. These gears can be mounted inside a cube or cuboid at 90 degrees so that one gear makes the other move.

To do this, the same strong triangles (axle holders) that were used to hold the axles on the chassis (see page 106) can be fixed

Equal gears fixed inside a cuboid to change the direction of movement

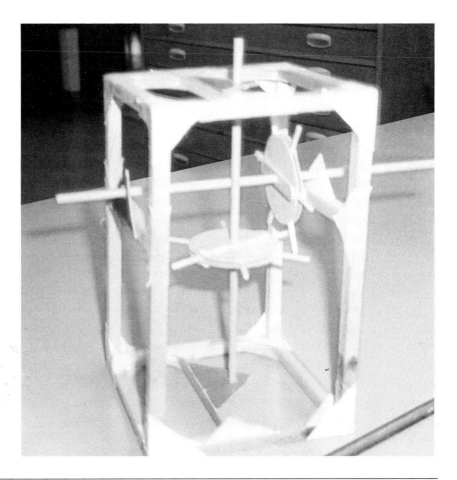

fixed on two opposite sides of the cuboid. The dowel on which the gear is fixed slots through these axle holders to hold the gear inside the cuboid. The second gear is fixed in the same way but across another two sides of the cuboid, to hold the gears at right angles to each other.

By moving the gears closer together or further apart, the pins will mesh and the gears will change the direction of movement through 90 degrees.

These gears within the cuboid could then be the working parts of a windmill or watermill.

Gears of different sizes to change the speed of movement

Gears for slowing down or speeding up movement should be in ratio – one with twice the diameter of the other.

1 gear – 5.4 cm diameter with 6 spokes.
1 gear – 10.8 cm diameter with 12 spokes.

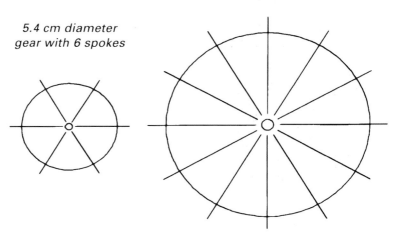

10.8 cm diameter gear with 12 spokes

5.4 cm diameter gear with 6 spokes

Two turns of the small gear = one turn of the larger gear.

Use lollipop sticks instead of matchsticks for these gears.

The small gear is made using the medium cardboard disc (54 mm). Place the disc on a geography grid divided into 10 degree sections and hold in place with masking tape.

Cut three straight lolly sticks in half, using either the hacksaw or Super Snips (beware of flying pieces).
Rub the edge of the sticks with glasspaper to remove the wax. This enables them to be stuck on their edge more easily.
Stick them onto the card disc at 60 degree angles using the grid as a guide, the straight cut just to the edge of the centre hole in the card disc.

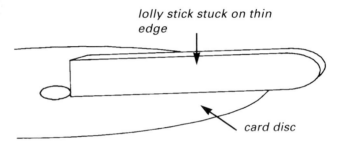

lolly stick stuck on thin edge

card disc

Complete the gear in the same way as for the equal gears.

To make the larger gear, you will need a circle of thick card with a diameter of 108 mm. This size of disc is now available but the alternative is to cut one out using an Olfa circle cutter. Gentle pressure and patience, using this cutter on a thick pad of newspaper or a cutting mat, will give good results.

As the diameter is twice the size of the small gear, use 12 whole, straight lolly sticks. Use the same grid as a guide, this time making the distance between the spokes 30 degrees.

The gear is made in the same way as the small one, sticking the lolly sticks on their edge after de-waxing.

You can see gears such as these on a hand drill or a food whisk. Turning the large gear once makes the small gear go round twice, which means that it goes round twice as fast

These gears, when fixed to a working model, will change the speed of movement.

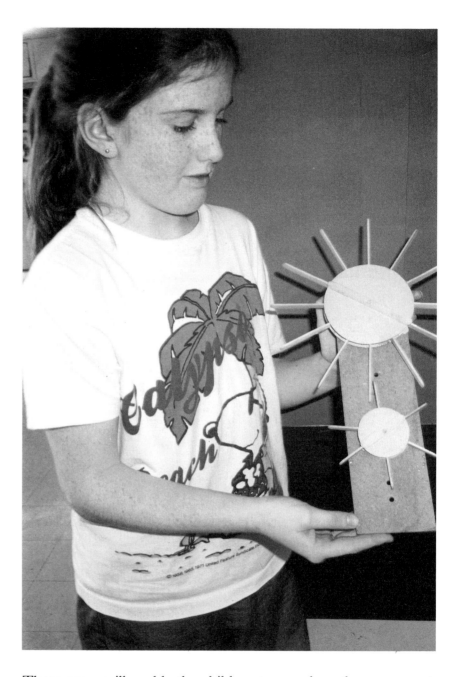

These gears will enable the children to speed up the movement on their models. They can be used to turn a turntable on a fire engine or crane and to speed up the movement of a roundabout.

8   Construction Kits

In order to develop with young children the skills and understanding of how things work, what makes things move and why some shapes are stronger and more rigid than others, it is necessary to ensure that they are given opportunities to work with both small- and large-scale construction kits as well as the materials available for their own model making.

When choosing constructional materials try to select kits that offer a wide range of opportunities for the children to fit shapes together in different ways (with pieces that push together, twist to fit, require nuts and bolts, etc) and to experience how parts such as gears, pulleys, winding devices, turntables and motors work.

The area in the classroom set aside for these materials could possibly be carpeted, both to designate the space and also reduce the noise level. Observing children working with these varied materials will enable you to ascertain the stages of development of the children in your care.

We can increase the value of construction kits by devising suitable activities and posing relevant questions. Free play alone may not lead to the appropriate concepts being developed. Time should be given for children to explore the kits with the teacher, in groups and on their own. Construction kits can be used in a wide variety of learning situations, together with other materials, as well as in problem solving.

Points to consider :
• Does a policy exist within school for the use of construction kits?
• Are construction kits generally available to all age-groups throughout the school?
• What specific vocabulary can be identified that the children will need to be aware of when using the kits?

The construction kit used must be of a level to develop the children's skills without being too different.

- Is the appropriate kit being used for the stage of development of the individual or group using it?
- Is there a policy for introducing new kits as the children progress?
- Are a variety of methods of construction used or do different kits use the same method, for example, push fit, twist, nuts and bolts, rods?
- Children may go through three distinct stages when using new kits:
  1 free play – to find out how pieces fit together
  2 copying from 2D pictures (supplied on the box or with the kit) to make 3D models
  3 making their own models based on their own ideas – these

may be quite simple at first, as the children become less reliant on the picture and more creative.

- Is it possible to organise a termly rota system so that a wide variety of construction kits can be fully used throughout school?
- Can a standardised system for the storing of kits be achieved? The storage of these materials is vital if they are to remain functional – a kit with only three wheels is not very helpful!

Evaluation of construction kits

The kits below have been organised in stages of experience rather than suitable age-ranges. If used in the order given, children will work through the skills possible in a structured way rather than beginning with a construction kit whose parts and demands are too complex for the beginner. The following evaluations are from teachers across the 4 to 11 age-range, after they had used the materials themselves and observed children's use of them.

NES house bricks
- Large, realistic plastic bricks with a simple interlinking system to enable the youngest children to build large, strong structures quickly.
- Ideal to link with children's work in other areas, for example, the homes of the three little pigs.
- Life-size material.
- Stacks, stores and cleans with ease.

Maxi Bricks
- Large, brightly coloured building bricks available in full and half sizes.
- They offer ideal opportunities for developing early building skills, tall structures, etc.

Duplo/Duplo Functions
- Highly recommended by teachers, they are used by infants only in most schools.
- The material also presents opportunities for older children to use in problem-solving activities.

Lego

- Many children have this at home. It should not be the only constructional toy.
- Versatile and useful throughout the primary age-range for structures, bridges, etc.
- This kit can be added to as much or as little as is needed.
- All parts can be replaced – extra wheels, pulleys, axles, etc

First Gear

- This new kit is very satisfying for very young children as it is good for small hands to manipulate.
- Colourful, attractive, versatile, easily assembled and very reasonably priced.
- A good introduction to basic technological concepts of gears and how they work.
- Fun to play with, sturdy, and although initially appealing to young children, it is suitable for a wider age-range.
- The kit can be used as parallel gears, speeding up and slowing down movement, or for changing movement through 90 degrees.
- It invites children to touch and explore and is aesthetically pleasing.
- This kit has been very well received by all who have worked with it (teachers, students and children).

Magnetic blocks

- Colourful and sturdy, interesting to look at.
- Easy for young children to handle, giving pleasing results.
- Suitable for imaginative play rather than construction techniques.
- A different first play introduction to magnets.
- Teachers felt that the material had limited use, did not extend the children far enough and that there were insufficient pieces.

Sticklebricks

- Good for the youngest children for beginning constructions.
- The pieces deteriorate fairly quickly.
- Very easy to use and provides instant results.
- Not much thought from the children needed but the very young (3–5 years) really enjoy this material.

Meccano – a challenging and enjoyable kit for older children.

- Ideal for creative and imaginative play.
- New kits broaden the possibilities with character heads, opening doors and windows.

Lasy

- Very versatile, fixes together well, good wheels which turn easily.
- This kit can be bought in three sizes – Jumbo, Maxi and Midi all of which fit each other.
- Includes lovely figures with moveable joints.
- There are additional extension packs for group/individual work.
- Contains motor and gears.

Plastic Meccano

- Bright, tough pieces in primary colours to attract young children.
- The kit helps the children to understand fixing by using nuts and bolts – tightening with a spanner.
- Help is given with an ideas sheet but the kit is also good for free construction use.
- Extra pieces including wheels can be purchased easily.

- All the pieces in this plastic kit link with the standard metal Meccano product.

Mobilo

- This kit is used widely in nursery/infant schools.
- Easy for young children to design models with wheels and axles.
- Assembles satisfyingly quickly.
- Attractive, brightly coloured pieces.
- Easy to find the required shape because they are always the same colour.
- The fasteners could be difficult as correct pressure has to be applied.
- Very versatile moving pieces – hinges, turntables, ladders, etc
- Lots of imaginative possibilities.
- More than one kit needed for groups of children.

Bauplay

- This was the first 'early years' kit to enable children to build models using gears of various sizes (see First Gear above).
- A large amount of this kit is necessary to enable maximum use.
- It is very expensive but the quality is superb.
- Brightly coloured, large pieces, very robust and very well used by the schools who have it.
- It can be purchased in smaller packs to spread the cost.
- Storage could be a problem for classrooms with limited space.
- Macrobit angle pieces fit it and also the Reo-Click wheels.

Reo-Click

- Wide range of possibilities; easy to fit together, not always so easy to take apart!
- Does not withstand chewing! Pieces can split. Tubes ideal for children to whistle down.
- An easy and exciting step between creative play and model making.
- Children enjoy using it.
- Comes in storage tub.
- Extension kit is available for older children.

Brio Mec

- Good. The only kit that has both wooden and plastic pieces and a tool kit.
- Has been available for a long time.
- Interesting and challenging with plenty of scope for developing the skills of screwing and hammering.
- The basic kit is less 'open ended' than many but new extension kits have been introduced to broaden the scope of the materials.

Macrobit

- Endless scientific and technological possibilities.
- Very sturdy, good size nuts and bolts.
- Children need to work together on a task – there are not enough pieces for many children to each make a large model.
- The models can be used by the children themselves – ridden, pushed, pulled.
- This is a kit that needs plenty of room for making and using as a working model.
- Expensive to purchase but excellent.

Tactic

- There was a very positive response from teachers on in-service training.
- It is felt that this material is too complicated for nursery children – the twist and lock and twist and pull actions are too hard for them to cope with.
- Much more successful with older children.
- More straight, yellow connectors would be a useful addition and would make the kit more versatile.
- Models can be as simple or as complicated as required.
- Large pieces which the children enjoy handling.
- Lovely if you have enough room in the classroom to leave the models on display – not suitable for a room with restricted space.

Fischertechnik

- Brightly coloured pieces in primary colours which fit together easily and very securely.

- At first on the market in Germany as a toy, this material is now being developed as an educational kit for learning skills and providing opportunities for creativity.
- It contains gears, ratchets, pulleys and different ways of fixing wheels and structures.
- This kit leads on to the well-established secondary kits which include pneumatics, hydraulics, etc.

Construx
- Good value for money, and highly recommended.
- Acts as a good middle stage between early kits and Lego Technic.
- Contains plenty of action pieces including hinges, pulleys, turntable devices and suction caps.
- The Power Creations pack includes an excellent motor – ideal for younger children, it enables models to move forward, lift, reverse and turn. This motor can be built into the model or used as a remote control.
- An excellent kit for use across the primary age-range.

Maxi Moduul
- Big, bold, quick and effective but would need a large quantity to build anything worthwhile.
- Attractive possibilities for life-size, stable constructions if there is enough space in the classroom.
- Fits together easily and is bright, colourful, strong.

Poly M
- The pieces can be a little stiff to put together for small fingers, as they need squeezing together quite firmly – this is more complicated than it at first appears.
- The kit extends imagination and language.
- It could serve the same purpose in the middle stages as Duplo in the early stages – building and fitting pieces together.
- Pleasant shapes with rounded edges.
- The little figures are a good idea.
- Bright, bold colours but the pieces are sometimes a little difficult to pull apart.

Quadro
- Large-scale, tubular construction kit secured safely by a simple locking screw.
- Ideal material for play house, slide, climbing frame, etc.
- Strong, weatherproof but lightweight.
- Suggested ages 6–10 years but younger children would love this material if their teacher helped make the model.
- Wheel kits are available but two kits are needed for a four wheeled model!
- Available also in a miniature size (Mini Quadro).

Teko
- Good for the child who has already had some experience of gears and how they work.
- Dull colour; perhaps more suited to the older child.
- Well-made pieces, providing lots of possibilities for creation and development of the children's own ideas.
- Links well with the requirements of the National Curriculum from Key Stage 2 onwards.
- Structures are quickly assembled, though there is insufficient wood in the standard kit to develop a variety of designs.
- Could perhaps be linked with other materials as children develop their understanding of working gears.
- Use of this kit before their own working model making would help the children's understanding of mechanisms.
- The motor is a useful addition and extension.
- This kit would extend children's first experiences with First Gear and Bauplay.

Lego Technic
- This is often the only kit for older children.
- Good for experience with pulleys, gears, levers and for identifying specific concepts (eg gear ratios).
- As Lego Technic is a material which many children have at home, their experience and expertise can be built upon.
- Can be too work card orientated – needs to be used in a more open-ended teaching situation.
- Endless possibilities for working with motors, linking with simple switching through to computer control (special Technic Control now available).

- An excellent kit but it must be built into a structured and staged experience for the children.
- It should not be their first experience of construction kits as the parts are very small and children need to have gained some understanding through experience with the earlier materials (First Gear, Bauplay and Teko).

Topic Technology with Older Children

Technology in the National Curriculum, March 1990 states clearly that:

Pupils should be taught to draw on their knowledge and skills in other subjects – to support their designing and making activities.

As teachers, we must encourage the children to recognise opportunities that already exist within the curriculum to develop their design-related activities. As we saw in Part 3, such activities can be identified from any of the following starting points:

> Stories and poems
> Topics and themes
> Mathematics
> Craft
> Science
> Music
> Visits
> Movement or PE
> Drama
> Computing
> Cooking
> Humanities
> Display
> Creative art
> Co-operative games
> World studies
> The children's own, first-hand experiences.

Brainstorming sessions with the children will highlight some of the opportunities for design-related activities.

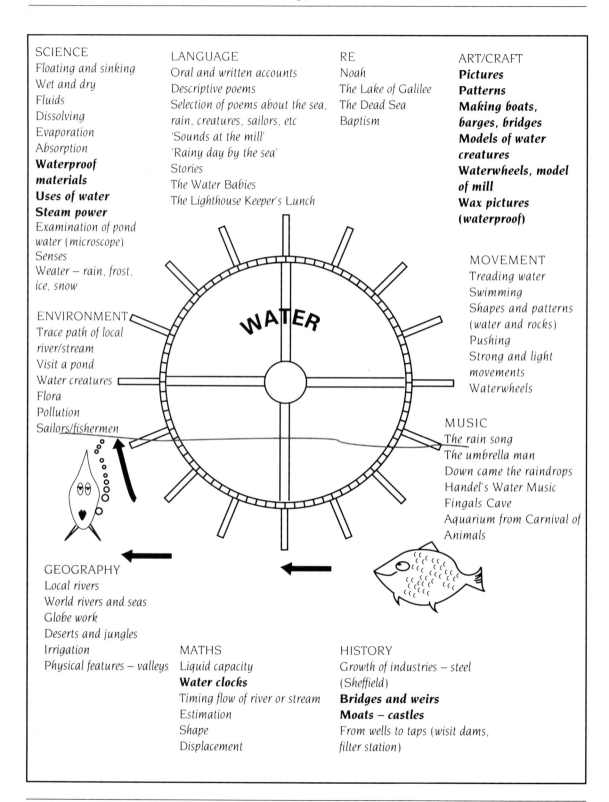

SCIENCE
Floating and sinking
Wet and dry
Fluids
Dissolving
Evaporation
Absorption
**Waterproof
materials**
Uses of water
Steam power
Examination of pond
water (microscope)
Senses
Weater – rain, frost,
ice, snow

ENVIRONMENT
Trace path of local
river/stream
Visit a pond
Water creatures
Flora
Pollution
Sailors/fishermen

GEOGRAPHY
Local rivers
World rivers and seas
Globe work
Deserts and jungles
Irrigation
Physical features – valleys

LANGUAGE
Oral and written accounts
Descriptive poems
Selection of poems about the sea,
rain, creatures, sailors, etc
'Sounds at the mill'
'Rainy day by the sea'
Stories
The Water Babies
The Lighthouse Keeper's Lunch

MATHS
Liquid capacity
Water clocks
Timing flow of river or stream
Estimation
Shape
Displacement

RE
Noah
The Lake of Galilee
The Dead Sea
Baptism

HISTORY
Growth of industries – steel
(Sheffield)
Bridges and weirs
Moats – castles
From wells to taps (wisit dams,
filter station)

ART/CRAFT
Pictures
Patterns
**Making boats,
barges, bridges**
**Models of water
creatures**
**Waterwheels, model
of mill**
**Wax pictures
(waterproof)**

MOVEMENT
Treading water
Swimming
Shapes and patterns
(water and rocks)
Pushing
Strong and light
movements
Waterwheels

MUSIC
The rain song
The umbrella man
Down came the raindrops
Handel's Water Music
Fingals Cave
Aquarium from Carnival of
Animals

WATER

The topic for the second term of a class of third year junior children, aged 9-10 years, was 'Water'. The teacher's plan is shown in the topic web on the previous page. Look how much technology was in this topic before it even existed as a curriculum area and without us even realising it! (The technology activities have been picked out in **bold** lettering.)

The starting point for this topic could have been any of the following:
- A visit to a water mill
- A rainy day
- A disaster at sea
- The Noah's Ark story
- A visit to the seaside
- A visit to the reservoir
- A visit to the water works

The starting point for this class was a visit to a working water mill at Worsbrough, South Yorkshire. The children were shown round the mill by the miller who asked them to pretend that they were sacks of grain. They were taken through the mill following the route of the grain as it goes through the milling process.

The sounds of the water as it ran over the wheel, the machinery clanging as the water sent the cogs round were all recorded on a tape recorder. The first-hand experiences of being covered with dust and smelling the atmosphere within the mill all led to the children's understanding of life in times gone by and the hard life of the poor miller. They made rough sketches of various parts of the mill while they were there and wrote down a list of the immediate highlights of their visit. Postcards, flour and souvenir pencils were purchased from the mill.

Back in the classroom the children planned the record of their visit. They had decided to make individual books and to include sketches, paintings and writing. Some of the writing was printed out on the computer, while other pieces

Opposite: Working model of a waterwheel with gears and pulleys

were handwritten. One group of children decided to try to make a working model of the mill. The building structure was the first piece to be made. This was then divided into floors to show how the grain had to be taken to the top of the mill to enable the process of milling to begin. Gears were made from corrugated card stuck round coffee jar lids of different sizes. The water wheel was made from dowel, wood and cardboard, all of which were polyurethane varnished to make them waterproof.

You can imagine the complexity of this work. It led the children to learn about pulleys for the sack hoist, gears for the grinding mechanism, the accuracy of fitting two grinding stones together and stopping the flour from shooting all over the mill.

This topic took place in 1985 and the above was the only technological activity we identified at the time. As our vision of technology has broadened with the implementation of the National Curriculum, other aspects of the topic can be seen to fit in under technological activities. The children used the flour they had bought to make bread, they made their bread into cottage loaves, bread cakes and rolls. They produced observational drawings of the mill as a whole and selected various mechanical sections to draw in detail. They painted posters to advertise the mill and these were displayed at the mill for other groups to see.

My second topic web shows clearly how much more technology can be drawn from the same topic if we are aware of the opportunities and plan for technology. The activities listed in the topic web are those identified by myself as a teacher. The list does not show technological activities identified by the children. I'm sure that many other possibilities will arise once the work of the topic is in progress. I hope that this example of topic planning will help you as an individual and also as a staff to broaden your thinking when planning and thus enable children to have the broad, balanced and relevant curriculum discussed in so many recent documents on primary education.

ENGLISH

Stories   Lighthouse Keepers Lunch
The Water Babies
Selection of stories and poems about the miller, water, the sea, the rain and sailors

Written work   Reporting – on visits
Creative – written, imaginative descriptions as story and poem – written or verbal planning to solve problem, describing functions/roles of yet-to-be-built machine/device
Instructing – logical planning of instructions, on completing a task, for use by other children

Language   Describing – the sounds, smells and work of a waterwheel
Evaluating – success/otherwise of solution to a problem, suggesting possible refinements/improvements

SCIENCE

Water and life – designing and building a school pond to sustain plants or minibeasts
Designing (probably verbally) suitable temporary accomodation for collected minibeasts
Resistance to water – designing and making waterproof clothes for dolls/people, testing for reliability and wearability
Damp courses in bricks; capillary action
Waterproofing roofs
Using rain gauges to keep record of rainfall over period of time
Visits – life in pond, stream, river, dam. Looking at
      buildings – shapes of roof

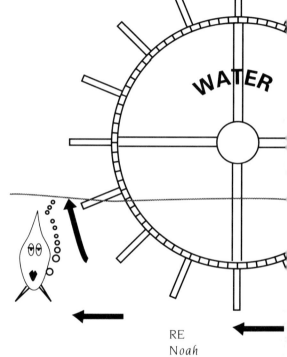

GEOGRAPHY

Local rivers, world rivers and seas
Globe work
Deserts and jungles
Irrigation
Physical features – valleys
Visits – reservoirs – purpose,
      function and construction
      the coast – erosion
      rivers and canals feeding
      watermills

MATHS

Capacity
Water clocks
Timing flow of river/stream
Estimating
Shape
Displacement
Measuring – designing rainfall measurers and testing them
(The last five activities could be listed under Science)

RE

Noah
The Lake of Galilee
The dead Sea
Jesus walking on the water

IT

Database – storing information
Working with the turtle
Printing their stories and poems
Designing logos for the mill

MUSIC/DRAMA
Production for other children on theme of WATER – planning, designing the theatre,
scenery, lighting, music, script, logical ordering and presentation
Handel's Water Music
Fingals Cave
Aquarium from Carnival of the Animals

COOKING
Use of flour in our diet – white, wholemeal
Make bread – other uses of bread, eg pizza
Other cooking using flour

MOVEMENT
Treading water
Swimming
Shapes and patterns (water and rocks)
Pushing
Strong and light movements
Waterwheels

TECHNOLOGY
Designing, building and evaluating different waterwheels using a wide range
of appropriate materials – extend by linking waterwheel to a mechanism
(gears, pulleys, link with construction kits
Design device for moving grain/flour
Design and make container to hold flour sold at mill
Design postcard/poster adverising mill/museum
Water patterns/colours
Reflections
Design for fabric of umbrells, taking into account shape and pattern
Design weather charts, using symbols
Design and make container for liquids
Design a device that uses water to lift a load
Making boats, barges, bridges
Models of water creatures

HISTORY
History of watermills
Growth of industries which need water
Bridges and weirs
Development of water industry – dams, filter and pumping stations
Visits –   railway museums (steam power)
           watermills (water power)
           waterworks (from sky to tap)

Appendix 1   Classroom Organisation

Looking at classroom space

Take a look at the space available in your classroom and how you are using it. It can be difficult to decide whether you are using your space effectively or not.

Maybe a possible starting point is to ask yourself the following questions:
- Do the children stay in one place for all their work?
- Do you operate an integrated day or a whole-class teaching approach?
- Do the children move about to various planned activity areas?
- Is your school open plan or classroom designed?
- Do you work individually, alongside colleagues or as part of a team?
- Are your rooms resourced individually or have you a centrally organised resource area?

Your answers to the above questions considered in relation to the following sections will help you to assess how space is utilised in your own classroom and school.

How can you create space?

- As an individual in your own classroom.

Use of floor space:
  - Do you have a carpeted area?
  - Do you have a wet or messy area?
  - Do you need a chair for each child?
  - Could grouping of furniture help?
  - Is stackable furniture available?
  - Could you make use of stacking trays or baskets?
  - Is there space for extra shelves or hanging space?
  - Could the hall, corridors, cloakrooms be used as additional areas?

- As part of a team.

In addition to the above ideas, if team teaching is taking place in two rooms:
  - Is it possible to organise one room with tables and chairs for writing, reading, language and number activities, using the second room as an open-plan area where children have space to work on creative activities, making use of the floor for construction kits, number games, etc?

This could also be considered if two teachers work in one large room.

- As a school.

  - Could ideas be shared in a brainstorming session?
  - Would it be advantageous to visit other schools to look at the different ways in which space has been used, taking photographs during these visits to help you to evaluate various classroom layout and different storage ideas?
  - Could advice be sought from advisory service or outside consultancy?

What do you need space for in technology?

- Practical activities – designing, making and testing
- Storage of tools and equipment
- Storage of unfinished work
- Storage of completed models
- Sundry items – sketching materials, record folders, paints, etc
- Displays

Creating an attractive classroom environment

The recommendation of the DES document *The Curriculum 5-16* is that:

Active learning and a sense of purpose and success enhances pupils' enjoyment, interest, confidence and a sense of personal worth. Passive learning and inappropriate teaching styles can lead to frustration and failure.

Creating the right classroom environment for technology means making it both organised and attractive.

This suggests that we should be concerned to create a facilitating learning situation and a classroom climate which promotes individual growth and communicates the joy of learning. At the early stages in childrens' development, it is unlikely that they need to be engaged in formal learning. Lack of formality, however, does not imply a lack of structure. The learning situation we want to create demands a high degree of organisation.

It is essential that the classroom is set out in an attractive and inviting way and that it is prepared in advance of the children's arrival each day. As children arrive they need to be able to go directly to activities. This would be an ideal opportunity for parents or grandparents to share in the life of the classroom.

Even in a traditional 'box' classroom, we can create areas for different categories of play and exploration.

Areas need to be provided for:
• natural materials
• creative activities
• construction kits

- writing and drawing
- structured play
- books
- jigsaws and table top games
- music and sound.

With very young children it is on the first three areas that we need to concentrate if we want the children to develop a technological awareness. The activities the children experience will encourage the creativity, inventiveness and problem-solving approach which is essential to early years technology.

Using your display

Displays, both in the classroom and around the school, provide opportunities to develop observational skills, as well as being stimulating (see pages 50–2). It is important that the work, whenever possible, is displayed within easy reach and view of the children. This is particularly important throughout the developmental stages of the work so that children involved in the making can share ideas with and demonstrate learning experiences to other pupils.

Consideration of the following questions should help you to create interactive displays.

- Is the display there for the children to touch?
- Is it within their reach?
- Do children respect each other's work on display?
- Could a standard framework set by the teacher give a starting point to the children for their own display; for example, attractively covered boxes with drapes for the children to use?
- Could the children design their own display?
- Do different year groups share each other's work?
- Is the display a talking point?
- Are children encouraged to play with displayed artefacts?
- Are they encouraged to continue working on displayed artefacts?

Appendix 1   Safety in the Classroom

I keep six honest serving men
They taught me all I know:
Their names are what and why and when
And how and where and who . . .
Rudyard Kipling

The above quotation applies to all aspects of our work with children but can be linked very appropriately to looking at the safe use of tools. If children are taught in the correct use of tools from an early age, the activity is safer and results in the teacher or adult present feeling less need for rigid supervision.

We should instil in children a sense of responsibility when using tools, so that they will always consider the following questions:

- **What** is the most appropriate tool for the task?
- **Why** have they chosen the particular tool?
- **When** should they use it?
- **How** should they use it?
- **Where** should they use it?
- **Who** is responsible for looking after the tool and storing it safely?

Pay special attention to the use of craft knives, glue guns, soldering irons and any power tools. In most schools with children below the age of 11, these items are for teacher use only and not readily available in the classroom for the children. The hot glue gun is a superb tool for applying glue to items where other glues have not been successful, and help children over a frustration point. However, the liquid glue which comes from the gun is very hot and can cause severe blistering if not used with great care, so should only be used by the teacher.
A new low melting point glue gun has just become available (see page 157). Craft knives have been banned in most primary

classrooms but, should they be there, a Maun steel safety rule must be the only ruler used in conjunction with the craft knife. This ensures that fingers are well away from the cutting blade. There is some concern regarding children working with polystyrene as it can produce a dust which collects in the lungs; an alternative material might be stryrofoam – an insulation material which has been tested and found to be safe. This material cuts very easily with the Shaper saw or hacksaw.`

Appendix 2   Evaluation

Evaluation is an important aspect of National Curriculum requirements and needs to be an ongoing process. Evaluation is concerned with what each child has actually learned from the design-related experiences undertaken. This includes the child's critical appreciation of the tasks set and the materials provided. You could use the following questions to help establish your own evaluation procedure.

Evaluating the activity

- Did each child achieve the objectives set?
- Would you set the same problem again? If yes, would it need modification. If no, could you say why?
- Did you record enough information about the experience for you or a colleague to plan future activities?
- Was the information recorded in such a way that it is easily accessible?

Evaluating the children

Questions to ask of each child:
- Did the child understand the problem?
- Did the child have enthusiasm and motivation to solve the problem?
- Was the problem resolved by:
  - trial and error?
  - drawing and designing?
  - negotiating?
  - looking for further information?
  - intuition?
  - a combination of the above?
- Did the child make an appropriate selection and use of materials and tools?
- Did the child modify their design after finding an initial solution?

- Did the child evaluate the process?
- Did the child make use of any the following technological concepts?
  - materials
  - structures
  - energy
  - control

This information can be recorded in any way you wish. You may consider collecting or photographing a selection of the children's early ideas and plans, models, drawings and writing, together with notes explaining the reasons for their choice.

One simple idea which has been very successful is to give the the children a notebook in which they can put down the problems as they encounter them, the materials they need for the next session, rough sketches to help them think through their problems – in fact, anything which they feel needs recording. This notebook is for their own use, not to be marked for spelling mistakes or untidy writing. When the project is over, there is then a child's record of the process through which they have gone. This record, together with the folder of their work as suggested in the previous paragraph, gives a comprehensive picture of technology in action. It is not possible to keep many finished models, space being required for the next activity, therefore photographs help to jolt the memory when open days arrive and assessment records appear.

For class records

Class records should include the following information:

- listing of topic themes, resources used, method/approach used and achievements
- aims
- objectives
- listing of concepts, skills, values and attitudes, knowledge, activities/experiences/cross-curricular links
- specific needs of individual children, for example:
  - needs challenge to extend

- needs more experience to reinforce
- needs more time to develop drawing skills
- should be encouraged to think more for him/herself
- needs to broaden the choice of materials
- encouragement required to use construction kits to help work out solutions
- must work with others to develop language skills and gain confidence
- needs persuasion to write about the activities undertaken
- must appreciate the aesthetic qualities of the finished work
- needs to be encouraged to talk about possible improvements/modifications to a solution.

Useful Addresses

Design, Craft and Graphics Ltd
Hanborough Business Park
Long Hanborough
Oxford OX7 2AB
Tel 0993 882588

A wide range of construction
materials including foamboard
and craft tools. Low melting point
glue guns.

Economatics Education Ltd
Epic House
Darnall Road
Attercliffe
Sheffield S9 5AA
Tel 0742 561122

Fischertechnik kits for children
from 8 years upwards,
Lego Dacta, tools and power
supplies.

Heron Educational
Unit 3
Carrwood House
Carrwood Road
Sheepbridge
Chesterfield S41 9QB
Tel 0246 453354

Resources include technology
trolley, First Gear and Magnetic
construction kits.

N.E.S. Arnold Ltd
17 Ludlow Hill Road
West Bridgford.
Nottingham NG2 6HD
Tel 0602 452200

All resources, including the widest
range of construction kits and
beads to fit 4.5 mm dowel.

P.E.L. Ltd.
Rood End Road
Olbery
Warleyt
West Midlands B69 4HN
Tel 021 5523377

All classroom furniture storage
units with plastic trays.

Primary Wood Supplies
Rotherham Road
Maltby
Rotherham S66 8ES
Tel 0709 814837

All resources, good prices for wood
packs, dowel. Speedy delivery.

Sheffield Purchasing Organisation
Staniforth Road
Sheffield S9 3GZ
Tel 0742 560424

A very wide range of resources
including construction kits,
materials and tools.

Surplus Buying Agency
Birley School
Fox Lane
Sheffield S12 4WU
Tel 0742 646186

An organisation which buys in bulk
surplus items and sells to schools at
good prices. Send for their list.

Technology Teaching Systems Ltd
Penmore House
Hasland Road
Chesterfield S41 0SJ
Tel 0246 278993

Wide range of equipment and
materials including electrics.

Bibliography

The Practical Curriculum, Schools Council Working Paper 50.

Primary Practice: a sequel to "The practical curriculum", Schools Council Working Paper 75.

Better Schools, DES, March 1985.

The Curriculum from 5 – 16 Curriculum Matters 2, DES, 1985.

Craft, Design & Technology from 5 – 16 Curriculum Matters 9, DES, 1987.

Primary Schools – some aspects of good practice, DES 1987. An HMI publication.

Design and Primary Education, The Design Council, March 1987.

A Language for Life, DES, 1975.

National Curriculum – Design & Technology 5-16 Proposals, DES, June 1989.

National Curriculum Council Consultation Report – Technology, NCC, November 1989.

Technology in the National Curriculum, DES, March 1990.

Primary Detail Design and Technology, Leeds LEA, 1990.

Science 5/13 series, *Structures and Forces*, Stages 1 and 2, Schools Council Pulication, MacDonald Educational, 1972.

Further Reading

Aitken and Mills, *Creative Technology*, Holmes Macdougall, 1987.

Elaine Baker, Brian Hillary, Chris Hillary, Steve Noon, Patricia Reiff, *Brain Waves: Towards Technology, Bridges, Primary Design*, Scholarstown Educational Publishers, 1989.

Andrew Breckon, *Introducing Craft, Design and Technology*, Thames/Hutchinson, 1983.

The Design Council, *The Big Paper*, can be purchased direct from the Design Council or from gook newsagents.

The Design Council Primary Education Working Party, *Design and Primary Education*, The Design Council, 1987.

Cyril Gilbert, Look! *Primary Technology*, Oliver & Boyd, 1987.

Mark Hiner, *Paper Engineering for Pop-up Books and Cards*, Tarquin Publications, 1985.

David Macaulay, *The Way Things Work*, Dorlin Kindersley.

Mary Horn Working Party, *Primary Science Working Papers 1–7*, Maths, Science and Technology Centre,Bristol, 1985–6.

Mills and Aitken, *Starting Technology Book 1*, Holmes Macdougall, 1984.

Questions Magazine, °Exploring Science and Technology 3–13, published monthly by Questions Publishing Co Ltd, 6/7 Hockley Hill, Birmingham B18 5AA.

David Rowlands and Carol Holland, *Problem-Solving in Primary Science and Technology*, Stanley Thornes, 1991.

SCSST and Engineering Council, *Problem Solving: Science and Technology in Primary Schools*, 1985.

Rainbow Technology, Key Stages 1 & 2, Stanley Thornes.